The Giant Book of Gripping Facts

by
Jake Jacobs

* * * * *

Published by Jake Jacobs

The Giant Book of Gripping Facts
Copyright© 2023 by Jake Jacobs

1.

Christopher Sower was a prominent German-American printer, publisher, and bookseller during the colonial era.

2.

He was born on September 26, 1693, in Laasphe, Germany.

3.

Sower was from a family of printers and publishers, and he learned the trade from his father.

4.

In 1724, Sower emigrated to America and settled in Germantown, Pennsylvania, which had a large German-speaking community.

5.

He established the first German printing press in Pennsylvania, which became one of the most successful and influential German-language presses in the American colonies.

6.

Sower's printing press played a crucial role in preserving and promoting German culture and language in America.

7.

He published a wide range of books, including religious texts, Bibles, hymnals, schoolbooks, and almanacs, catering to the needs of the German-speaking population.

8.

Sower's printing shop was a center for intellectual and cultural exchange, attracting scholars, writers, and thinkers from both Europe and America.

9.

He was known for his meticulous attention to detail and high-quality craftsmanship, producing books that were highly regarded for their accuracy and beauty.

10.

Sower's printing press became a vital tool for the dissemination of knowledge and information among German-speaking communities in America.

11.

He was a strong advocate for education and established a German-English school in Germantown, where he taught and provided educational resources.

12.

Sower's publications played a significant role in shaping the religious and intellectual landscape of the German-American community.

13.

He printed the first German-language Bible in America, known as the "Germantown Bible" or the "Sower Bible," which was a landmark achievement in American printing history.

14.

Sower's Bible was highly esteemed for its accuracy and readability and became widely used by German-speaking communities.

15.

He was a vocal supporter of the Moravian Church and published many religious texts and hymnals for the Moravian community.

16.

Sower's printing press also produced a variety of non-religious works, including historical accounts, political writings, and scientific treatises.

17.

His publications played a role in shaping public opinion during the American Revolution, disseminating revolutionary ideas and promoting the cause of independence.

18.

Sower's commitment to the principles of the Enlightenment is evident in the range of subjects he published, which covered science, philosophy, and literature.

19.

He faced challenges and censorship during the colonial period, as some of his publications were deemed controversial or politically sensitive.

20.

Sower's influence extended beyond Germantown and had an impact on German-speaking communities throughout the American colonies.

21.

He established a family printing dynasty, and his sons, Christopher Sower Jr. and Peter Sower, continued the family business after his death.

22.

Sower's printing press continued to operate for over a century, playing a significant role in preserving and promoting German language and culture in America.

23.

He was a proponent of a "plain style" of printing, emphasizing clarity, simplicity, and readability in his publications.

24.

Sower's printing press was a vital link between German-speaking communities in America and the broader intellectual and cultural movements of the time.

25.

He contributed to the development of a distinctly German-American identity, fostering a sense of community and shared heritage among German immigrants.

26.

Sower's publications often included illustrations and engravings, showcasing the artistic and technical skills of his printing shop.

27.

He was known for his innovation and experimentation in printing techniques, using different typefaces, layouts, and ornamentation to enhance the visual appeal of his books.

28.

Sower's printing shop employed skilled craftsmen, including type founders, engravers, and bookbinders, creating a vibrant hub of artistic and technical expertise.

29.

He actively participated in the cultural life of Germantown, supporting local institutions, churches, and community organizations.

30.

Sower's printing press was a catalyst for the development of a German-language literary tradition in America, fostering the growth of German-American literature.

31.

He contributed to the preservation of German folk traditions and folktales, publishing collections of stories, songs, and customs.

32.

Sower's publications provided practical knowledge and information on various subjects, including agriculture, medicine, and trade, catering to the needs of the German-American settlers.

33.

He established a wide network of correspondents and collaborators, exchanging ideas and information with other printers and intellectuals in Europe and America.

34.

Sower's printing press also produced materials for the Pennsylvania Dutch community, including almanacs, broadsides, and pamphlets.

35.

He faced financial challenges at times, as the cost of importing paper and type from Europe was high, and competition from English-language printers was fierce.

36.

Sower's publications had a lasting impact on the development of German-language printing in America, inspiring and influencing subsequent generations of printers and publishers.

37.

He was an advocate for religious freedom and tolerance, promoting dialogue and understanding among different religious denominations.

38.

Sower's printing press played a crucial role in the transmission of German-language culture and literature to future generations of German-Americans.

39.

He was a visionary entrepreneur, recognizing the potential of the German-language market and successfully meeting the needs of a growing immigrant population.

40.

Sower's legacy as a printer and publisher continues to be celebrated today, and his publications are highly sought after by collectors and historians.

41.

He was a multifaceted intellectual, engaging with a wide range of subjects and ideas, reflecting the diversity and richness of his printing output.

42.

Sower's printing press contributed to the growth of literacy and education among German-speaking communities, empowering individuals with knowledge and information.

43.

He believed in the transformative power of books and the importance of intellectual freedom in fostering social progress.

44.

Sower's commitment to excellence and professionalism in printing elevated the standards of German-language printing in America.

45.

He supported the abolitionist movement and used his printing press to disseminate anti-slavery literature and promote social justice.

46.

Sower's printing press was a vital tool for preserving and promoting the German language in America, especially during a time when English-language dominance was increasing.

47.

He maintained strong connections with his European roots, importing books and materials from Germany and maintaining an active correspondence with European publishers and intellectuals.

48.

Sower's printing press contributed to the development of a distinct German-American literary tradition, fostering the growth of poetry, fiction, and non-fiction in the German language.

49.

He encouraged and supported the development of young writers and intellectuals, providing a platform for their work in his publications.

50.

Sower's contributions to the American printing industry and his role in preserving German language and culture make him a significant figure in the history of American publishing and the German-American community.

51.

Friedrich Wilhelm August Heinrich Ferdinand von Steuben, commonly known as Baron von Steuben, was born on September 17, 1730, in Magdeburg, Prussia (now Germany).

52.

He came from a family of minor Prussian nobility and was the son of Royal Prussian Engineer Capt. Wilhelm Augustin von Steuben.

53.

Von Steuben began his military career at the age of 17 when he joined the Prussian Army.

54.

He served as an officer in the Seven Years' War and fought in several battles, including the Battle of Prague and the Battle of Torgau.

55.

Von Steuben rose through the ranks of the Prussian Army, eventually attaining the position of captain.

56.

He had a reputation as a skilled and disciplined military officer, known for his organizational abilities and attention to detail.

57.

In 1763, after the end of the Seven Years' War, von Steuben was discharged from the Prussian Army due to budget cuts.

58.

Following his discharge, von Steuben faced financial difficulties and struggled to find a new military position.

59.

In 1777, von Steuben met Benjamin Franklin in Paris, France, who introduced him to George Washington and the American cause for independence.

60.

Impressed by von Steuben's military experience, Washington recommended him to the Continental Congress as a potential asset to the Continental Army.

61.

Von Steuben arrived in America in 1777 and offered his services to the Continental Army as a volunteer.

62.

He initially faced skepticism from American military leaders due to his lack of fluency in English and the foreign nature of his background.

63.

Von Steuben was appointed as a Major General and was assigned the task of training and disciplining the Continental Army at Valley Forge during the winter of 1777-1778.

64.

Using his extensive military experience, von Steuben developed a comprehensive training program for the soldiers, focusing on drills, tactics, and discipline.

65.

He wrote a drill manual, commonly known as the "Blue Book" or the "Regulations for the Order and Discipline of the Troops of the United States," which became the standard drill manual for the Continental Army.

66.

Von Steuben's training methods and discipline significantly improved the efficiency and effectiveness of the Continental Army.

67.

He played a crucial role in transforming the Continental Army from an undisciplined and poorly trained force into a professional fighting force.

68.

Von Steuben's influence extended beyond training; he also contributed to the development of military regulations, logistics, and the establishment of a standardized organizational structure.

69.

He advocated for the establishment of an inspector general's office to maintain discipline and standards within the army.

70.

Von Steuben was known for his strict discipline and rigorous training methods, but he also had a reputation for fairness and impartiality.

71.

He was highly respected and admired by the soldiers he trained, who affectionately referred to him as the "Baron."

72.

Von Steuben played a key role in the success of the Continental Army in the later stages of the American Revolutionary War.

73.

He participated in several significant battles, including the Battle of Monmouth and the Siege of Yorktown.

74.

Von Steuben's contributions to the American Revolution were recognized and appreciated by the Continental Congress and military leadership.

75.

In 1784, von Steuben was granted U.S. citizenship by an act of the Continental Congress.

76.

After the war, von Steuben retired from the military and settled in New York State, where he lived on a small estate.

77.

He was known for his hospitality and frequently hosted social events at his estate, including dinners and parties.

78.

Von Steuben never married and did not have any children.

79.

He maintained close friendships with many American military leaders, including George Washington and Alexander Hamilton.

80.

Von Steuben's legacy extended beyond his military contributions; he was a proponent of a strong centralized government and was involved in the early stages of drafting the U.S. Constitution.

81.

He supported the establishment of a standing army and the creation of a Department of War.

82.

Von Steuben was appointed as one of the original members of the Society of the Cincinnati, an organization formed by officers of the Continental Army.

83.

He remained active in veterans' affairs and supported efforts to improve the welfare of soldiers and veterans.

84.

Von Steuben's contributions to the American Revolution were recognized by several European nations, and he received honors and decorations from Prussia, France, and the Netherlands.

85.

He published a memoir titled "Regulations for the Order and Discipline of the Troops of the United States," detailing his experiences and insights on military training and discipline.

86.

Von Steuben's training methods and drill techniques continued to be influential in the U.S. Army long after the American Revolution.

87.

He is often referred to as the "Father of the U.S. Military Training."

88.

Von Steuben's statue stands in Lafayette Square in Washington, D.C., honoring his significant contributions to the American military.

89.

His legacy is also commemorated through various schools, streets, and parks named after him throughout the United States.

90.

Von Steuben's impact on the Continental Army helped shape the development of a professional military force in the newly formed United States.

91.

He is considered one of the most influential military figures of the American Revolution.

92.

Von Steuben's contributions to the American cause for independence were essential in turning the tide of the war and securing victory.

93.

His training methods and emphasis on discipline and organization set a standard for future generations of American military leaders.

94.

Von Steuben's dedication to the American cause and his commitment to training and discipline earned him the respect and admiration of his contemporaries.

95.

He passed away on November 28, 1794, in his estate in Utica, New York, at the age of 64.

96.

Von Steuben's burial site is located in the Steuben Memorial State Historic Site in Remsen, New York.

97.

The legacy of Baron von Steuben as a military strategist and trainer continues to be studied and celebrated by historians and military scholars.

98.

His contributions to the American Revolution helped shape the outcome of the war and the establishment of the United States as a sovereign nation.

99.

Von Steuben's story exemplifies the impact that foreign-born individuals had on the success of the American Revolution.

100.

His dedication, expertise, and passion for military training left an indelible mark on the history of the United States, earning him a place among the great figures of the American Revolution.

101.

Brandling worms, scientifically known as Eisenia fetida, are a species of earthworm commonly used in vermicomposting.

102.

They are also referred to as tiger worms, red wigglers, or manure worms.

103.

Brandling worms are native to Europe but have been introduced to various regions worldwide for their composting capabilities.

104.

These worms have a cylindrical body with a characteristic reddish-brown color, which distinguishes them from other earthworm species.

105.

Brandling worms are hermaphroditic, meaning they possess both male and female reproductive organs.

106.

They reproduce by laying egg capsules known as cocoons, which contain multiple embryos.

107.

The cocoons are small, lemon-shaped structures that are typically deposited in the organic matter or soil.

108.

Brandling worms are highly efficient composters and play a crucial role in breaking down organic waste materials.

109.

They feed on decaying organic matter, such as vegetable scraps, fruit peels, coffee grounds, and shredded paper.

110.

The digestive process of brandling worms helps to convert organic waste into nutrient-rich vermicompost.

111.

Vermicompost produced by brandling worms is a valuable fertilizer, rich in nutrients, beneficial microorganisms, and organic matter.

112.

The vermicompost produced by brandling worms is often used to enrich soil, improve plant growth, and enhance soil fertility.

113.

Brandling worms have a voracious appetite and can consume their own body weight in organic waste each day.

114.

They have a preference for moist environments and thrive in bedding materials such as shredded paper, cardboard, or compost.

115.

Brandling worms have a unique ability to tolerate a wide range of environmental conditions, including temperature fluctuations.

116.

They can survive temperatures between 32°F (0°C) and 95°F (35°C), although they are most active in temperatures between 60°F (15°C) and 80°F (27°C).

117.

Brandling worms have a relatively short lifespan, usually ranging from 1.5 to 2 years.

118.

They have a significant impact on soil health and structure through their burrowing activity, which improves aeration and water infiltration.

119.

Brandling worms are excellent indicators of soil health. Their presence in the soil indicates a well-balanced and fertile ecosystem.

120.

These worms have a symbiotic relationship with certain bacteria and microorganisms in their digestive system, aiding in the decomposition process.

121.

Brandling worms have been used in vermiculture for centuries, with evidence of their use dating back to ancient civilizations..

122.

Vermiculture, the practice of using worms for composting, is an eco-friendly and sustainable method of waste management.

123.

The castings or excreta produced by brandling worms are highly concentrated in plant nutrients, enzymes, and beneficial microorganisms.

124.

Vermicomposting with brandling worms produces compost that is superior in quality to traditional composting methods.

125.

The castings produced by brandling worms contain high levels of humus, which improves soil structure, water retention, and nutrient availability.

126.

Vermicomposting with brandling worms is suitable for both small-scale and large-scale applications, such as home gardens, community gardens, and commercial farms.

127.

These worms are highly adaptable and can thrive in various vermicomposting systems, including compost bins, vermiculture beds, and worm towers.

128.

Brandling worms are an integral part of the natural decomposition process in ecosystems, aiding in the breakdown of organic matter in forests and grasslands.

129.

Their activity helps to recycle nutrients, improve soil fertility, and support the growth of plants in natural environments.

130.

Brandling worms are commonly used in vermiculture to compost kitchen scraps, garden waste, and other organic materials that would otherwise end up in landfills.

131.

They have a remarkable ability to process and neutralize certain pathogens and pathogens present in organic waste, reducing the risk of disease transmission.

132.

The excretions of brandling worms contain plant growth-promoting substances, such as auxins and cytokinins, which stimulate root development and enhance plant growth.

133.

Vermicomposting with brandling worms reduces greenhouse gas emissions compared to traditional composting methods, as it facilitates faster decomposition and minimizes anaerobic conditions.

134.

These worms are sensitive to light and prefer dark environments. They will burrow deeper into the soil or bedding material if exposed to excessive light.

135.

Brandling worms have a positive impact on the overall biodiversity of the soil ecosystem by enhancing microbial diversity and providing a food source for other organisms.

136.

They have a minimal ecological footprint and do not pose any significant threats to the environment or native ecosystems.

137.

Brandling worms have been successfully used in the restoration of degraded soils, helping to revitalize the soil structure and improve its fertility.

138.

The movement and burrowing activity of brandling worms enhance soil aggregation, which contributes to better soil stability and erosion control.

139.

Vermicomposting with brandling worms can help reduce the volume of waste sent to landfills, promoting waste reduction and recycling.

140.

These worms can adapt to a wide range of organic materials, making them suitable for composting various types of organic waste, including paper waste, animal manure, and agricultural residues.

141.

Brandling worms are commercially available for vermicomposting purposes and can be purchased from specialized suppliers or worm farms.

142.

Vermicomposting with brandling worms is a sustainable practice that aligns with the principles of organic farming and gardening.

143.

These worms exhibit a behavior known as "worm casting migration," where they move to areas with the freshest organic matter to feed and deposit their cocoons.

144.

Brandling worms are highly efficient at breaking down organic materials, and their presence in a composting system can accelerate the composting process significantly.

145.

They have been used in vermiculture research and studies to explore their potential in waste management, soil remediation, and sustainable agriculture.

146.

Brandling worms have a natural aversion to acidic conditions, and their presence in soil can help regulate pH levels by increasing alkalinity.

147.

Vermicomposting with brandling worms is an accessible and educational activity for children and adults alike, promoting environmental awareness and sustainability.

148.

These worms are sensitive to temperature fluctuations and will seek shelter in cooler or warmer areas to regulate their body temperature.

149.

Brandling worms have been introduced to various regions around the world to enhance soil fertility and promote sustainable agricultural practices.

150.

Vermicomposting with brandling worms is a continuous and cyclical process, as new generations of worms are continually hatching and replacing older individuals, ensuring a constant composting capacity.

151.

The Brazilian Wandering Spider, scientifically known as Phoneutria, is a highly venomous spider found in Central and South America, particularly in Brazil.

152.

It is considered one of the most venomous spiders in the world and is known for its aggressive behavior.

153.

The Brazilian Wandering Spider is named for its habit of wandering rather than building a traditional web.

154.

It belongs to the family Ctenidae and is closely related to other wandering spiders found in the Americas.

155.

The spider has a leg span of up to 6 inches (15 centimeters) and a body length of around 2 inches (5 centimeters).

156.

It has a distinctive appearance with a brown or dark brown body and long, slender legs.

157.

The Brazilian Wandering Spider is known for its strong neurotoxic venom, which can cause severe pain, muscle spasms, and even death in some cases.

158.

The venom of the Brazilian Wandering Spider contains a potent neurotoxin called PhTx3, which affects the nervous system.

159.

The venom can cause priapism in males, a painful and prolonged erection that can last for several hours.

160.

While extremely venomous, the Brazilian Wandering Spider rarely bites humans unless provoked or threatened.

161.

When threatened, the spider raises its front legs and displays its fangs as a warning signal.

162.

The Brazilian Wandering Spider is a nocturnal hunter and feeds on insects, other spiders, small reptiles, and sometimes even small mammals.

163.

It has excellent vision and is able to detect movement and prey from a distance.

164.

The spider's fangs are large and strong, allowing it to deliver a powerful bite to immobilize its prey.

165.

Female Brazilian Wandering Spiders are larger and more venomous than males.

166.

Males are known for their courtship behavior, which involves a complex series of drumming and leg movements to attract a female.

167.

After mating, the female lays eggs in a silk sac and guards them until they hatch.

168.

The eggs hatch into spiderlings, and the female carries them on her back for protection until they are ready to disperse.

169.

Brazilian Wandering Spiders are adaptable and can thrive in a variety of habitats, including forests, grasslands, and urban areas.

170.

They are often found in dark and sheltered places, such as under rocks, in tree bark, or inside human structures.

171.

The spider has a strong affinity for bananas, and incidents of Brazilian Wandering Spiders hiding in banana shipments have been reported.

172.

The bite of a Brazilian Wandering Spider can cause symptoms such as intense pain, sweating, increased blood pressure, irregular heartbeat, and even respiratory distress.

173.

Immediate medical attention is required if bitten by a Brazilian Wandering Spider, as the venom can be potentially lethal.

174.

Antivenom is available for treating bites from the Brazilian Wandering Spider, and prompt administration can be life-saving.

175.

The Brazilian Wandering Spider's venom has attracted scientific interest due to its potential therapeutic applications, particularly in the treatment of erectile dysfunction.

176.

Research is ongoing to study the properties of the venom and develop medications based on its components.

177.

Despite its venomous nature, the Brazilian Wandering Spider plays a role in the ecosystem by controlling populations of insects and other small arthropods.

178.

The spider's aggressive behavior and venomous reputation have made it the subject of many urban legends and myths.

179.

The Brazilian Wandering Spider has been featured in popular culture, appearing in movies, books, and video games.

180.

It is often depicted as a dangerous and menacing creature due to its potent venom and aggressive nature.

181.

The Brazilian Wandering Spider has natural predators, including birds, snakes, and larger spiders.

182.

The spider has specialized hairs on its legs, known as urticating hairs, which it can flick at potential threats to deter them.

183.

In addition to its venomous bite, the Brazilian Wandering Spider can also deliver a painful bite without injecting venom.

184.

The spider has a strong grip and is capable of scaling vertical surfaces and even hanging upside down.

185.

Brazilian Wandering Spiders have a lifespan of around 3-4 years in the wild.

186.

Their ability to adapt to urban environments has led to increased encounters between humans and these spiders.

187.

Brazilian Wandering Spiders have complex mating rituals that involve specific movements and vibrations to communicate with potential mates.

188.

The spider's venom affects the nervous system by disrupting the transmission of nerve signals.

189.

The Brazilian Wandering Spider's venom is being studied for its potential use in pain management and the development of new medications.

190.

The venom of the Brazilian Wandering Spider has been found to contain compounds that can act as a potent insecticide.

191.

The spider is known to be highly sensitive to vibrations, allowing it to detect potential threats or prey.

192.

The Brazilian Wandering Spider has been used in scientific research to study the mechanisms of venom action and explore potential applications in medicine.

193.

It has a unique ability to adjust its venom composition depending on the type of prey it encounters.

194.

Brazilian Wandering Spiders have specialized structures on their legs called tarsi pads, which allow them to cling to surfaces with great strength.

195.

The spider's venom is not only neurotoxic but also cytotoxic, causing damage to cells and tissues at the bite site.

196.

The Brazilian Wandering Spider has a wide distribution in Brazil, including the Amazon rainforest, Cerrado savanna, and Atlantic Forest.

197.

Due to its venomous nature, the Brazilian Wandering Spider is often considered a dangerous pest in areas where it comes into contact with humans.

198.

The spider's aggressive behavior and potent venom have led to it being listed as a species of medical importance in Brazil.

199.

Efforts are underway to educate the public about the risks associated with the Brazilian Wandering Spider and to promote measures for prevention and control.

200.

Despite its reputation, the Brazilian Wandering Spider plays an important ecological role in maintaining the balance of insect populations and contributing to the biodiversity of its natural habitat.

201.

Daisy Bates House is a historic landmark located in Little Rock, Arkansas, United States.

202.

The house was the residence of civil rights activist Daisy Bates and her husband, L.C. Bates.

203.

It is a two-story, red brick house that was built in 1893.

204.

The house is located at 1207 West 28th Street in Little Rock's West 28th Street Historic District.

205.

Daisy Bates House served as the headquarters for the Arkansas State Conference of the National Association for the Advancement of Colored People (NAACP) during the Civil Rights Movement.

206.

The house played a significant role in the desegregation of Central High School in Little Rock in 1957.

207.

Daisy Bates, as the president of the Arkansas NAACP, guided the nine African American students known as the "Little Rock Nine" in their efforts to integrate the previously all-white Central High School.

208.

The house provided a safe meeting space for civil rights leaders, activists, and supporters during the tumultuous times of the Civil Rights Movement.

209.

Daisy Bates House became a center of strategic planning and coordination for the battle against racial segregation in Arkansas.

210.

The house was a refuge for the Little Rock Nine students, who often sought solace and support there during the challenging integration process.

211.

Daisy Bates House was also a hub for organizing legal strategies, rallies, and protests aimed at achieving equal rights and opportunities for African Americans in Arkansas.

212.

The Bateses held numerous meetings and events at their house, gathering activists, attorneys, community leaders, and journalists to discuss civil rights issues and plan actions.

213.

The Bateses faced threats, intimidation, and violence due to their prominent role in the Civil Rights Movement, but they remained steadfast in their commitment to equality.

214.

The Bateses' home became a symbol of courage, resilience, and determination in the face of racial discrimination.

215.

The house's historical significance was recognized when it was listed on the National Register of Historic Places in 1986.

216.

In 2001, the house was designated a National Historic Landmark for its association with the events of the Civil Rights Movement.

217.

The Daisy Bates House now serves as the Daisy Bates State Memorial, commemorating the life and legacy of Daisy Bates.

218.

The memorial includes exhibits and displays that highlight Daisy Bates' activism, the Little Rock Nine, and the struggle for civil rights in Arkansas.

219.

Visitors can explore the house and learn about the pivotal role it played in the fight against segregation.

220.

The memorial serves as an educational resource, offering insights into the challenges faced by African Americans during the Civil Rights Movement.

221.

The Daisy Bates State Memorial stands as a testament to the power of grassroots activism and the impact of individuals in effecting social change.

222.

The house's architecture reflects the Queen Anne style, featuring decorative woodwork, a wraparound porch, and distinctive windows.

223.

The interior of the house has been preserved to reflect the time when the Bateses lived there.

224.

The rooms contain period furnishings, photographs, and memorabilia related to the Civil Rights Movement.

225.

The Daisy Bates State Memorial offers guided tours that provide in-depth information about the Bateses' contributions to the struggle for civil rights.

226.

The memorial serves as an important resource for researchers, historians, and scholars studying the Civil Rights Movement.

227.

Daisy Bates House continues to inspire and educate visitors about the ongoing struggle for equality and social justice.

228.

The Bateses' commitment to civil rights extended beyond the Little Rock Nine, as they fought for equal voting rights, access to public facilities, and fair housing for African Americans.

229.

Daisy Bates House serves as a reminder of the sacrifices made by activists like Daisy Bates and the immense courage it took to challenge segregation and systemic racism.

230.

The house stands as a living monument to the progress made in the fight for civil rights and the work that still needs to be done.

231.

The Daisy Bates State Memorial hosts special events, lectures, and exhibits that explore various aspects of the Civil Rights Movement.

232.

The memorial welcomes visitors from all backgrounds, fostering dialogue and understanding about the importance of equality and inclusivity.

233.

The Daisy Bates State Memorial is part of the Arkansas Civil Rights Heritage Trail, which recognizes significant sites associated with the struggle for civil rights in the state.

234.

The memorial contributes to the preservation of African American history and culture in Arkansas.

235.

The Bateses' legacy continues to inspire activism and advocacy for social justice in Little Rock and beyond.

236.

The Daisy Bates House and memorial are maintained and managed by the Arkansas State Archives.

237.

The house's location in the West 28th Street Historic District adds to its historical context, as the district encompasses other significant structures from the early 20th century.

238.

The Bateses' house served as a gathering place for African American community members seeking support, guidance, and resources during a time of racial discrimination.

239.

Daisy Bates House represents the power of grassroots organizing and community mobilization to bring about lasting change.

240.

The Bateses' contributions to civil rights were recognized with numerous awards and honors, including the Spingarn Medal from the NAACP in 1958.

241.

The memorial serves as a tribute to the countless unnamed individuals who fought for civil rights alongside the Bateses and the Little Rock Nine.

242.

The house's location in the heart of Little Rock allows visitors to explore the city's broader civil rights history and the ongoing efforts for racial justice.

243.

Daisy Bates House has become an important site for pilgrimage, where visitors pay homage to the brave individuals who stood up against segregation.

244.

The memorial encourages dialogue about the persistence of racial disparities and the need to continue the fight for equality.

245.

The house's preservation and transformation into a memorial demonstrate the importance of preserving historical landmarks and recognizing their cultural and social significance.

246.

The Bateses' activism and the significance of their home have been documented in books, documentaries, and academic studies.

247.

The Daisy Bates State Memorial offers educational programs and workshops for students, promoting a deeper understanding of civil rights history and inspiring future leaders.

248.

The memorial's exhibits showcase the evolution of civil rights activism and highlight the ongoing struggle for equality in America.

249.

Daisy Bates House represents the collective power of individuals and communities to effect change, even in the face of immense adversity.

250.

The preservation of Daisy Bates House and its transformation into a memorial ensure that the legacy of Daisy Bates and the Civil Rights Movement remains alive for future generations.

251.

Bathhouse Row is a collection of historic bathhouses located in Hot Springs National Park, Arkansas.

252.

It is situated along Central Avenue, the main street in downtown Hot Springs.

253.

Bathhouse Row is a designated National Historic Landmark District, recognized for its architectural and historical significance.

254.

The district consists of eight bathhouses, all constructed between 1892 and 1923.

255.

The bathhouses were built to capitalize on the natural hot springs in the area, which were believed to have healing properties.

256.

Each bathhouse on Bathhouse Row offered different spa treatments and services, catering to various preferences and health needs.

257.

The architecture of the bathhouses is predominantly neoclassical, reflecting the grandeur and elegance of the era.

258.

The most iconic bathhouse on Bathhouse Row is the Fordyce Bathhouse, which now serves as the visitor center for Hot Springs National Park.

259.

The Fordyce Bathhouse is open to the public and offers guided tours, allowing visitors to step back in time and experience the opulence of the early 20th century.

260.

The bathhouses on Bathhouse Row were known for their elaborate marble interiors, stained glass windows, and ornate fixtures.

261.

Each bathhouse had a unique design and atmosphere, offering a variety of bathing and spa experiences.

262.

The water used in the bathhouses is sourced from the thermal springs in Hot Springs National Park, which maintain a constant temperature of around 143°F (62°C).

263.

Hot mineral water from the springs was believed to have therapeutic properties and was used for bathing, drinking, and other treatments.

264.

The bathhouses also offered additional amenities such as steam rooms, saunas, massages, and exercise facilities.

265.

Bathhouse Row was a popular destination for wealthy individuals seeking relaxation, rejuvenation, and socializing.

266.

During the peak of their popularity, the bathhouses attracted visitors from around the country, including famous personalities and politicians.

267.

The popularity of the bathhouses declined in the mid-20th century with the rise of modern medicine and changes in societal preferences.

268.

In the 1980s, efforts were made to revitalize Bathhouse Row and preserve its historical significance.

269.

The bathhouses underwent extensive renovations to restore their original charm and architectural features.

270.

Today, some of the bathhouses on Bathhouse Row are still in operation, offering spa treatments and services.

271.

Buckstaff Bathhouse is one of the bathhouses that has remained in continuous operation since its construction in 1912.

272.

The Superior Bathhouse, another bathhouse on Bathhouse Row, has been converted into a brewery and restaurant, combining history and craft beer.

273.

The Quapaw Baths and Spa is a modern facility that offers a contemporary spa experience while preserving the architectural beauty of the past.

274.

The Ozark Bathhouse now serves as the park's cultural center, hosting art exhibits and cultural events.

275.

The Hale Bathhouse is currently being renovated and will soon house the Hot Springs National Park headquarters.

276.

Bathhouse Row is surrounded by the natural beauty of Hot Springs National Park, with hiking trails and scenic vistas.

277.

The hot springs in the area were originally revered by Native American tribes, who believed in their healing powers.

278.

The U.S. government designated the area as a national reservation in 1832 to protect the hot springs.

279.

Hot Springs National Park was established in 1921, making it the oldest national park maintained by the National Park Service.

280.

Bathhouse Row and the surrounding area of Hot Springs National Park offer numerous opportunities for outdoor activities, including hiking, camping, and wildlife viewing.

281.

The area's natural hot springs are unique in the United States and draw thousands of visitors each year.

282.

The hot springs in Hot Springs National Park are among the few in the world that are located within a city.

283.

The water from the hot springs is odorless and tasteless, as it contains dissolved minerals but no sulfur.

284.

The thermal water from the hot springs is constantly replenished by rainwater that seeps into the ground and is heated by geothermal activity.

285.

The temperature of the hot springs varies from bathhouse to bathhouse, allowing visitors to choose their preferred level of heat.

286.

The hot springs in Hot Springs National Park are protected and regulated to ensure their preservation for future generations.

287.

The water from the hot springs is monitored regularly to maintain its quality and safety for bathing.

288.

Hot Springs National Park covers an area of approximately 5,550 acres (2,243 hectares) and encompasses both Bathhouse Row and the surrounding natural landscape.

289.

The park offers scenic drives, picnic areas, and opportunities for birdwatching and wildlife photography.

290.

The park's trails range from easy walks to more challenging hikes, providing options for visitors of all fitness levels.

291.

The historic Arlington Hotel, which overlooks Bathhouse Row, is a notable landmark in the area and has hosted many famous guests over the years.

292.

Hot Springs National Park is home to a variety of plant and animal species, including the endangered Ouachita rock pocketbook mussel.

293.

The park's thermal waters have been used for therapeutic purposes for centuries and continue to attract people seeking relief from various ailments.

294.

The hot springs were an important aspect of the cultural and social fabric of the local community, providing a gathering place for residents.

295.

Hot Springs National Park is located in the Ouachita Mountains, a region known for its scenic beauty and outdoor recreational opportunities.

296.

The park offers interpretive programs, guided hikes, and educational exhibits to enhance visitors' understanding of the area's natural and cultural history.

297.

The annual Hot Springs Documentary Film Festival, one of the oldest documentary film festivals in North America, takes place in Hot Springs National Park.

298.

Bathhouse Row and Hot Springs National Park have been featured in movies, television shows, and documentaries, showcasing their unique history and natural beauty.

299.

The preservation and restoration efforts of Bathhouse Row have been recognized with numerous awards and accolades.

300.

Bathhouse Row stands as a testament to the rich heritage of Hot Springs and its ongoing commitment to preserving its cultural and natural treasures.

301.

Richard Stockton was a prominent American lawyer, jurist, and statesman who lived from 1730 to 1781.

302.

He was born into a wealthy family in New Jersey and received an excellent education, including attending the College of New Jersey (now Princeton University).

303.

Stockton studied law and was admitted to the bar in 1754, establishing himself as a respected attorney.

304.

He gained fame for his eloquence and legal expertise, becoming one of the most renowned lawyers in New Jersey.

305.

Stockton served as a delegate to the Continental Congress from 1776 to 1777, representing New Jersey.

306.

He was a strong advocate for American independence and played an active role in the early stages of the Revolutionary War.

307.

Stockton signed the Declaration of Independence in 1776, pledging his commitment to the cause of American independence from British rule.

308.

In 1776, he was appointed to the New Jersey Supreme Court and became the first Chief Justice of the state.

309.

As Chief Justice, Stockton worked to establish the foundations of the New Jersey legal system and ensure justice and fairness.

310.

Stockton was a strong supporter of religious freedom and played a crucial role in drafting the New Jersey Constitution of 1776, which included protections for religious liberty.

311.

Despite his dedication to the American cause, Stockton faced personal difficulties during the Revolutionary War.

312.

In 1776, he was captured by the British and imprisoned, suffering physical and emotional hardships while in captivity.

313.

Stockton's health deteriorated during his imprisonment, and he was eventually released in 1777 as part of a prisoner exchange.

314.

Upon his release, Stockton returned to his home in New Jersey and continued his legal and political career.

315.

He was elected to the New Jersey legislature in 1777 and played a role in shaping the state's post-war government.

316.

Stockton was a strong advocate for the abolition of slavery and proposed legislation to gradually emancipate enslaved individuals in New Jersey.

317.

He also supported the establishment of public education and contributed to the development of the state's educational system.

318.

Stockton was an active member of the Society of the Cincinnati, an organization founded by officers of the Continental Army.

319.

In addition to his legal and political pursuits, Stockton was also a successful writer and philosopher.

320.

He wrote numerous essays and treatises on various subjects, including law, government, and the nature of human rights.

321.

Stockton was known for his eloquent speeches and persuasive writing style, which earned him a reputation as an influential and skilled orator.

322.

His writings often emphasized the importance of individual liberties, limited government, and the rule of law.

323.

Stockton's commitment to the principles of liberty and justice influenced his legal decisions and political advocacy.

324.

He believed in the power of reason and the pursuit of truth, and his writings often reflected his philosophical beliefs.

325.

Stockton's contributions to the development of American legal and political thought have had a lasting impact on the nation's history.

326.

He was a founding member of the American Philosophical Society, an organization dedicated to the promotion of knowledge and scientific inquiry.

327.

Stockton's devotion to public service and his commitment to the ideals of the American Revolution earned him the respect and admiration of his peers.

328.

He was known for his integrity, fairness, and dedication to the principles of justice.

329.

Stockton's untimely death at the age of 50 cut short a promising career and deprived the nation of a brilliant legal mind and statesman.

330.

He passed away on February 28, 1781, in Princeton, New Jersey.

331.

Stockton's legacy continues to be celebrated and honored in New Jersey and throughout the United States.

332.

His former residence, known as Morven, is now a museum that preserves his memory and showcases the history of the Revolutionary era.

333.

Stockton's descendants have also played prominent roles in American history, including his son Richard Stockton Jr., who became a U.S. Senator.

334.

The city of Stockton, California, is named after Richard Stockton, recognizing his contributions to the founding of the United States.

335.

Numerous schools, parks, and buildings across the country bear his name, commemorating his significant role in American history.

336.

Stockton's life and career continue to inspire scholars and researchers, who study his writings and contributions to American jurisprudence.

337.

His dedication to the principles of liberty and justice serve as a reminder of the ideals upon which the United States was founded.

338.

Stockton's story highlights the sacrifices made by the founding generation in their pursuit of freedom and self-governance.

339.

His experiences as a prisoner of war underscore the challenges faced by those who fought for independence during the Revolutionary War.

340.

Stockton's commitment to the abolition of slavery demonstrates his belief in the inherent equality and dignity of all individuals.

341.

His efforts to promote education and knowledge reflect his belief in the importance of an educated and enlightened citizenry.

342.

Stockton's writings on law and government provide valuable insights into the principles and ideas that shaped the early American legal system.

343.

He was an influential figure in the formation of the New Jersey state government and played a vital role in its early development.

344.

Stockton's contributions to the Continental Congress helped solidify the unity and resolve of the American colonies in their fight for independence.

345.

He was known for his ability to bridge divides and find common ground, making him an effective advocate and negotiator.

346.

Stockton's commitment to religious freedom reflects the broader struggle for religious liberty in the early American colonies.

347.

His role as Chief Justice of New Jersey laid the foundation for the state's legal system and the principles of fairness and justice it upholds.

348.

Stockton's imprisonment and subsequent release symbolize the sacrifices made by many in the pursuit of American independence.

349.

His writings on individual rights and limited government continue to be studied and debated by legal scholars and political theorists.

350.

Richard Stockton's life and contributions serve as a reminder of the courageous individuals who laid the groundwork for the United States and fought for the principles that define it today.

351.

Thomas Stone was a prominent American lawyer, planter, and politician who lived from 1743 to 1787.

352.

He was born in Charles County, Maryland, and grew up on his family's plantation known as "Haber de Venture."

353.

Stone received a classical education and attended the College of William and Mary in Virginia.

354.

After completing his education, he studied law and was admitted to the Maryland bar in 1764.

355.

Stone quickly established a successful legal practice and gained a reputation for his intelligence and integrity.

356.

He became involved in local politics and was elected to the Maryland Provincial Assembly in 1768.

357.

Stone was a staunch advocate for colonial rights and was active in the resistance against British policies leading up to the American Revolution.

358.

In 1774, Stone attended the First Continental Congress as a delegate from Maryland, where he worked alongside other prominent patriots.

359.

He continued to serve in the Continental Congress throughout the Revolutionary War, playing a vital role in shaping American independence.

360.

Stone was a signer of the Declaration of Independence in 1776, affixing his signature to the historic document.

361.

He was one of four Maryland delegates to sign the Declaration, alongside Samuel Chase, William Paca, and Charles Carroll.

362.

Stone's signature on the Declaration of Independence is known for its distinctive and elaborate flourish.

363.

During the Revolutionary War, Stone served as a member of the Continental Army, actively supporting the cause of American independence.

364.

He participated in the defense of Maryland against British forces during the Battle of Long Island in 1776.

365.

Stone's military service demonstrated his dedication to the revolutionary cause and his willingness to put himself in harm's way.

366.

After the war, Stone returned to his legal practice and served as a judge in the Maryland Court of Appeals.

367.

He was elected to the Maryland State Senate in 1783 and played a role in shaping the state's post-war government.

368.

Stone was a strong advocate for individual liberties and was instrumental in drafting Maryland's state constitution.

369.

He believed in the separation of powers and worked to establish a system of checks and balances within the Maryland government.

370.

Stone married Margaret Brown in 1768, and they had three children together.

371.

Margaret Stone was a devoted partner and supporter of her husband's political career.

372.

Despite his contributions to American independence, Stone's health declined in the years following the Revolutionary War.

373.

He suffered from numerous health issues, including severe asthma, which affected his ability to participate actively in politics.

374.

Stone retired from public life in 1785 and focused on his personal affairs and the management of his plantation.

375.

He passed away on October 5, 1787, at the age of 44, in Alexandria, Virginia.

376.

Stone was buried at his family's plantation, but the exact location of his grave is unknown.

377.

In recognition of his contributions to American history, the Thomas Stone National Historic Site was established in Maryland in 1978.

378.

The historic site preserves Stone's home, known as "Haber de Venture," and provides insights into his life and legacy.

379.

Stone's home showcases 18th-century plantation life and offers a glimpse into the personal and political world of the Founding Fathers.

380.

Stone's commitment to the cause of American independence and his role as a signer of the Declaration of Independence are commemorated at the site.

381.

Stone's signature on the Declaration of Independence solidified his place in American history and his commitment to liberty and self-governance.

382.

He was known for his intelligence, legal acumen, and devotion to the principles of the American Revolution.

383.

Stone's political career and contributions to the formation of the United States continue to be studied by historians and scholars.

384.

His writings and speeches provide valuable insights into the political and intellectual climate of the Revolutionary era.

385.

Stone's beliefs in individual rights, limited government, and the rule of law align with the broader ideals of the Founding Fathers.

386.

His dedication to public service and his willingness to sacrifice for the cause of American independence serve as an inspiration to future generations.

387.

Stone's commitment to justice and fairness is reflected in his work as a lawyer and his advocacy for a fair legal system.

388.

He was respected by his peers and held in high regard for his wisdom, integrity, and moral character.

389.

Stone's contributions to the American Revolution and the establishment of the United States are honored in various ways, including monuments, historical markers, and educational programs.

390.

His legacy as a Founding Father and a defender of American liberty continues to be celebrated and remembered.

391.

Stone's life and career highlight the important role played by lesser-known Founding Fathers in shaping the nation's history.

392.

He was a representative of the emerging professional class in colonial America, combining legal expertise with a commitment to public service.

393.

Stone's story illustrates the challenges faced by individuals who dedicated themselves to the cause of American independence.

394.

His experiences during the Revolutionary War and his subsequent contributions to Maryland's government demonstrate the complexities of nation-building.

395.

Stone's commitment to the ideals of the American Revolution was rooted in his belief in the fundamental rights of individuals and the principles of self-governance.

396.

He was known for his persuasive speaking abilities and his ability to articulate complex ideas in a clear and concise manner.

397.

Stone's contributions to the Maryland State Senate and the drafting of the state's constitution have had a lasting impact on the state's legal and political system.

398.

His work as a judge in the Maryland Court of Appeals helped shape the state's legal precedents and ensure the fair administration of justice.

399.

Stone's legacy as a Founding Father and a signer of the Declaration of Independence solidifies his place among the nation's most influential leaders.

400.

His commitment to the principles of liberty, justice, and self-determination continue to resonate with Americans today, serving as a reminder of the enduring ideals upon which the United States was founded.

401.

British mice, also known as the common house mouse (Mus musculus), are small rodents that are found throughout the United Kingdom.

402.

They are known for their adaptability and ability to thrive in a variety of environments, including urban areas, farmland, and woodlands.

403.

British mice have a lifespan of about one to two years in the wild, although some individuals may live longer under favorable conditions.

404.

They are typically light brown or gray in color, with a slender body, large ears, and a long tail.

405.

British mice have a keen sense of hearing and can produce a wide range of vocalizations, including squeaks, chattering, and ultrasonic calls.

406.

They are excellent climbers and can scale vertical surfaces with ease, aided by their sharp claws and flexible bodies.

407.

British mice are primarily nocturnal, meaning they are most active during the night and spend their days in nests or burrows.

408.

They are omnivorous, feeding on a varied diet that includes seeds, grains, fruits, insects, and even small invertebrates.

409.

British mice are prolific breeders and can produce multiple litters throughout the year, with each litter consisting of four to eight pups.

410.

The gestation period for British mice is around 19 to 21 days, and the newborn pups are blind and hairless.

411.

Mice have a rapid reproductive rate, which allows their populations to increase quickly under favorable conditions.

412.

They are known for their ability to squeeze through tiny openings and gaps, thanks to their flexible bodies and collapsible skeletons.

413.

British mice are excellent swimmers and can traverse bodies of water such as rivers, ponds, and ditches.

414.

Mice have a strong sense of smell, which they use to navigate their environment, locate food, and communicate with each other.

415.

They mark their territories and communicate through scent markings, urine, and pheromones.

416.

British mice are known to construct nests made of shredded materials such as paper, fabric, or vegetation, which they use for shelter and raising their young.

417.

Mice have well-developed teeth that continuously grow throughout their lives. Gnawing on hard objects helps them wear down their teeth.

418.

British mice have a highly developed sense of touch, particularly in their whiskers, which they use to navigate and explore their surroundings.

419.

They are agile and can perform acrobatic feats, such as leaping, balancing, and running along narrow ledges or wires.

420.

Mice have been associated with human settlements for thousands of years, often seeking shelter and food in homes, barns, and other structures.

421.

They can cause damage to buildings by gnawing on wires, insulation, and structural materials.

422.

British mice have a wide range of predators, including domestic cats, birds of prey, foxes, and snakes.

423.

They have a remarkable ability to memorize and navigate complex environments, enabling them to find their way back to food sources or nests.

424.

Mice are curious animals and will explore new objects or changes in their environment, often exhibiting neophobia (fear of new things) at first.

425.

British mice have been extensively studied in scientific research, particularly in the fields of genetics, behavior, and neuroscience.

426.

They have been used as model organisms in laboratory research due to their biological similarities to humans and their ability to reproduce quickly.

427.

Mice play a crucial role in medical research, contributing to advancements in the understanding and treatment of diseases such as cancer, diabetes, and neurological disorders.

428.

The field of genetics has greatly benefited from studying mice, as they share a significant portion of their genome with humans.

429.

British mice have a remarkable ability to navigate complex mazes and remember the locations of rewards, making them valuable subjects for studying learning and memory.

430.

They are also used in behavioral studies to investigate social interactions, aggression, and communication.

431.

British mice have been domesticated and kept as pets for centuries, providing companionship and entertainment.

432.

Domesticated mice come in a variety of colors and patterns, thanks to selective breeding by enthusiasts and breeders.

433.

Mice are highly social animals and display complex social hierarchies within their colonies.

434.

They communicate using a combination of vocalizations, body postures, scent markings, and tactile interactions.

435.

Mice are known for their playful behavior, engaging in activities such as chasing, wrestling, and jumping.

436.

They have excellent spatial memory and can remember the location of food sources or hidden objects over extended periods.

437.

Mice have been trained to perform a variety of tasks in scientific experiments, including maze navigation, lever pressing, and operant conditioning.

438.

British mice have a well-developed immune system and can mount robust immune responses against pathogens.

439.

They are used in vaccine development and testing to evaluate the efficacy and safety of new immunizations.

440.

Mice have contributed significantly to our understanding of the genetics of diseases and have helped identify numerous disease-associated genes.

441.

They have been instrumental in the development of gene-editing technologies, such as CRISPR-Cas9, which allow scientists to manipulate specific genes and study their functions.

442.

Mice have a remarkable ability to regenerate certain tissues, such as skin and liver, which has implications for regenerative medicine research.

443.

They have been used in studies on aging and age-related diseases, providing insights into the biological processes that underlie the aging process.

444.

Mice are an integral part of ecological research, as they play crucial roles in ecosystems as seed dispersers and prey for predators.

445.

They have a significant impact on crop production, as they can consume and contaminate stored grains and other agricultural products.

446.

British mice exhibit a wide range of behaviors, including nesting, burrowing, grooming, and territorial marking.

447.

They have a highly developed sense of balance, enabling them to move swiftly and gracefully across different surfaces.

448.

Mice possess excellent spatial awareness and can quickly learn and navigate complex mazes or environments.

449.

They are known for their ability to detect and respond to changes in their environment, including the presence of predators or potential threats.

450.

British mice, with their adaptability, intelligence, and scientific significance, continue to fascinate researchers, pet owners, and those interested in understanding the intricate workings of the natural world.

451.

British moles, scientifically known as Talpa europaea, are small, burrowing mammals native to the United Kingdom.

452.

They have a cylindrical body, covered in velvety black fur, with tiny eyes and ears that are often concealed within their fur.

453.

Moles are highly adapted for a subterranean lifestyle, with powerful front limbs and shovel-like hands perfectly designed for digging.

454.

British moles are solitary animals and spend the majority of their lives underground, rarely coming to the surface.

455.

They construct intricate tunnel systems called molehills, which consist of a network of interconnected passages used for foraging, nesting, and protection.

456.

The tunnels created by moles aerate the soil, helping with water drainage and promoting nutrient circulation.

457.

Moles have an acute sense of touch, aided by specialized sensory hairs on their bodies, which allow them to navigate and detect prey underground.

458.

They primarily feed on earthworms, but also consume other invertebrates, including insects, larvae, and small snails.

459.

Moles have a voracious appetite and can eat their body weight in food each day.

460.

British moles are primarily active during the night, spending the daytime hours resting in their burrows.

461.

They have a high metabolic rate and require a constant intake of food to sustain their energy levels.

462.

Moles have excellent hearing, which enables them to detect vibrations and sounds produced by prey or potential predators.

463.

They possess a highly developed sense of smell, which helps them locate prey and detect intruders in their tunnel systems.

464.

Moles communicate through a combination of vocalizations, scent markings, and tactile cues.

465.

Male moles are known to be territorial and will aggressively defend their burrows from other males.

466.

British moles have a complex mating system, with males engaging in aggressive courtship rituals to attract females.

467.

After mating, females construct spherical nests lined with grass and leaves to give birth to their young.

468.

Moles typically have one to two litters per year, with each litter consisting of three to five pups.

469.

The pups are born blind and hairless, but they develop quickly and are weaned within a few weeks.

470.

Moles have a relatively short lifespan of about three to four years in the wild.

471.

They are preyed upon by various predators, including owls, hawks, foxes, and domestic cats.

472.

Moles are well adapted for their underground lifestyle, with tiny eyes that are protected by a layer of skin to prevent soil particles from entering.

473.

The front paws of moles have an extra thumb-like digit called a "hand," which helps them in digging and manipulating soil.

474.

Moles can dig extensive tunnel systems that span several meters in length and depth.

475.

They create distinct molehills on the surface of the ground, which are composed of soil excavated from their tunnels.

476.

The shape and size of molehills can vary, depending on the species and the depth of the tunnels.

477.

Molehills play a role in aerating the soil and can serve as habitats for other animals, such as insects and small mammals.

478.

Moles are known for their remarkable digging speed, capable of burrowing at a rate of about 4 meters per hour.

479.

They have powerful muscles in their neck and shoulders, which allow them to exert force while pushing through compacted soil.

480.

Moles have adapted to a diet high in earthworms, as they provide a nutritious and easily accessible food source underground.

481.

They have specialized teeth designed for gripping and crushing their prey, allowing them to consume worms quickly and efficiently.

482.

Moles possess a remarkable ability to navigate underground, relying on a combination of touch, smell, and memory to find their way through their intricate tunnel systems.

483.

Their tunnels are typically located in grassy areas, meadows, gardens, and woodland edges.

484.

Moles are considered beneficial for gardens and agricultural fields, as they help control pests by consuming large numbers of soil-dwelling insects and larvae.

485.

Their burrowing activity can also improve soil fertility and structure by mixing and incorporating organic matter.

486.

Mole tunnels can serve as conduits for water, helping to prevent soil erosion and aiding in the distribution of rainfall.

487.

Moles are known to exhibit seasonal variations in their behavior, with increased activity during the breeding season and reduced activity during colder months.

488.

They have a unique circulatory system that allows them to survive in low-oxygen environments while burrowing underground.

489.

Moles are not hibernators but may retreat to deeper parts of their burrows during harsh winter conditions.

490.

Their fur is dense and waterproof, providing insulation and protection from the dampness of the soil.

491.

Moles have been the subject of study and fascination for centuries, with their remarkable adaptations and secretive lifestyle capturing the curiosity of scientists and nature enthusiasts.

492.

British moles have been featured in literature, folk tales, and children's stories, often depicted as industrious and tenacious creatures.

493.

The presence of molehills in the landscape can be indicative of healthy soil ecosystems and biodiversity.

494.

Molehills are sometimes used by other small animals as shelter or as a source of food, as they may contain insects and earthworms.

495.

Moles are well suited to their underground existence, with their streamlined bodies and lack of external ears reducing resistance while burrowing.

496.

They have a specialized gland in their body that produces a musky scent, which they use for marking their territory.

497.

Moles have a relatively low body temperature, allowing them to conserve energy while underground.

498.

Mole populations can fluctuate in response to factors such as food availability, weather conditions, and predation pressure.

499.

Moles are generally non-aggressive towards humans and will avoid direct contact whenever possible.

500.

Despite their subterranean lifestyle, British moles play an essential role in shaping and maintaining the ecological balance of their habitats, highlighting the interconnectedness of species within ecosystems.

501.

The Camden Expedition Sites are historical locations associated with the American Civil War's Camden Expedition, which took place in 1864.

502.

The expedition was a Union military campaign led by Major General Frederick Steele with the goal of capturing the Confederate stronghold of Camden, Arkansas.

503.

The Camden Expedition Sites include various locations in Arkansas, such as Poison Springs, Marks' Mills, Jenkins' Ferry, and Elkins' Ferry.

504.

Poison Springs, located in Ouachita County, was the site of a significant battle on April 18, 1864. Union forces suffered heavy casualties and were forced to retreat, while Confederate troops secured a victory.

505.

Marks' Mills, situated in Cleveland County, was the site of another major battle on April 25, 1864. Union forces were again defeated, resulting in significant losses for the Union Army.

506.

Jenkins' Ferry, located in Grant County, was the site of a pivotal engagement on April 30, 1864. Union forces successfully crossed the Saline River under heavy fire, allowing them to escape Confederate pursuit.

507.

Elkins' Ferry, situated in Clark County, was a critical crossing point on the Little Missouri River during the Camden Expedition. Union forces successfully crossed the river, evading Confederate opposition.

508.

The Camden Expedition was part of a larger Union strategy to secure control of the Red River region in Arkansas and Louisiana.

509.

The Union's ultimate objective was to disrupt Confederate supply lines, gain control of important waterways, and weaken the Confederacy's hold on the region.

510.

The Camden Expedition faced numerous challenges, including difficult terrain, unfavorable weather conditions, and determined Confederate resistance.

511.

Confederate General Sterling Price led the defense against the Union forces during the Camden Expedition, employing guerilla tactics and utilizing knowledge of the local terrain.

512.

The battles and skirmishes of the Camden Expedition resulted in significant casualties on both sides and had a lasting impact on the course of the Civil War in the region.

513.

The Camden Expedition demonstrated the challenges faced by Union forces in conducting large-scale military operations in the rugged and heavily forested areas of southern Arkansas.

514.

Many of the Camden Expedition Sites have been preserved and are now part of the Camden Expedition Sites National Historic Landmark.

515.

The Camden Expedition Sites provide valuable insights into the military strategies, tactics, and experiences of both Union and Confederate forces during the Civil War.

516.

The battlefields and related sites offer opportunities for historical interpretation, allowing visitors to learn about the soldiers, commanders, and local communities affected by the conflict.

517.

The Camden Expedition Sites also serve as a reminder of the sacrifices made by soldiers on both sides and the profound impact of the Civil War on the nation's history.

518.

The preservation of the Camden Expedition Sites contributes to the understanding and commemoration of the Civil War era and its significance in shaping the United States.

519.

The Camden Expedition represents one of the largest military campaigns conducted in Arkansas during the Civil War.

520.

The campaign was part of the broader Union effort to exert control over the Confederate-held territories in the Trans-Mississippi Theater.

521.

The Camden Expedition aimed to disrupt Confederate supply lines and weaken their military presence in the region.

522.

The battles fought during the expedition demonstrated the fierce determination and resilience of both Union and Confederate forces.

523.

The Camden Expedition Sites offer opportunities for archaeological research and the study of military strategies employed during the Civil War.

524.

Many of the sites have markers, monuments, or interpretive signs that provide historical context and information for visitors.

525.

The Camden Expedition Sites attract Civil War enthusiasts, historians, and researchers interested in studying the conflict and its impact on Arkansas.

526.

The sites allow visitors to walk in the footsteps of soldiers who fought in the Camden Expedition, providing a tangible connection to the past.

527.

The Camden Expedition played a role in shaping the outcome of the Civil War in Arkansas and contributed to the overall Union victory.

528.

The Confederate victories at Poison Springs and Marks' Mills boosted morale among Confederate troops and temporarily halted the Union advance.

529.

The Union victory at Jenkins' Ferry allowed them to regroup and ultimately continue their campaign.

530.

The Camden Expedition highlighted the challenges faced by both Union and Confederate forces in the unforgiving terrain of southern Arkansas.

531.

The expedition involved not only military engagements but also logistical challenges, including the need to maintain supply lines and coordinate troop movements.

532.

The Camden Expedition Sites showcase the diversity of landscapes in Arkansas, including forests, rivers, and rolling hills.

533.

The battles fought during the Camden Expedition demonstrated the importance of strategic positioning and the use of natural features in military campaigns.

534.

The sites offer opportunities for reflection and contemplation, allowing visitors to consider the human cost of war and the impact it had on local communities.

535.

The Camden Expedition Sites serve as a reminder of the complex and multifaceted nature of the Civil War, with its political, social, and economic implications.

536.

The Camden Expedition Sites contribute to the broader understanding of the Civil War as a transformative period in American history.

537.

The sites provide educational resources and materials for students and teachers studying the Civil War and its impact on Arkansas.

538.

The Camden Expedition Sites are managed and preserved by various entities, including state and local historical societies, preservation organizations, and government agencies.

539.

The preservation of the Camden Expedition Sites helps protect and conserve the region's historical and cultural heritage for future generations.

540.

The sites offer opportunities for guided tours, interpretive programs, and reenactments that bring the history of the Camden Expedition to life.

541.

The battles fought during the Camden Expedition were characterized by moments of bravery, sacrifice, and resilience on the part of soldiers on both sides.

542.

The Camden Expedition had a significant impact on the local civilian population, with many residents being directly affected by the conflict.

543.

The expedition brought attention to the strategic importance of Arkansas as a battleground and a vital region for both Union and Confederate forces.

544.

The Camden Expedition Sites contribute to ongoing research and scholarship on the Civil War, helping to expand our knowledge and understanding of this pivotal period in American history.

545.

The Camden Expedition Sites demonstrate the ways in which historical events and landscapes are interconnected, highlighting the importance of preserving and interpreting these sites.

546.

The Camden Expedition Sites have the potential to contribute to heritage tourism and local economic development by attracting visitors interested in the Civil War and history.

547.

The Camden Expedition Sites offer opportunities for outdoor recreational activities, such as hiking, bird-watching, and picnicking, in addition to their historical significance.

548.

The Camden Expedition Sites are part of a broader network of Civil War sites and historical landmarks throughout the United States, contributing to a comprehensive understanding of the conflict.

549.

The preservation and interpretation of the Camden Expedition Sites require ongoing collaboration among historians, archaeologists, local communities, and government agencies.

550.

The Camden Expedition Sites stand as a testament to the courage, sacrifice, and enduring legacy of the individuals who participated in the campaign, reminding us of the profound impact of the Civil War on the nation's history.

551.

The Eaker Site is an archaeological site located in northeast Arkansas, United States.

552.

It is named after Carl and Pauline Eaker, who discovered the site in the 1960s while plowing their field.

553.

The Eaker Site is associated with the Late Mississippian culture, which thrived in the region between 1000 and 1500 AD.

554.

It is believed to have been a village site occupied by the Nodena people, a Native American culture of the Mississippian period.

555.

The site is situated on a bluff overlooking the Mississippi River, providing strategic and advantageous views of the surrounding area.

556.

Archaeological excavations at the Eaker Site have revealed a wealth of artifacts, including pottery, tools, weapons, and ceremonial objects.

557.

The pottery found at the site displays intricate designs and motifs, showcasing the artistic skills of the Nodena people.

558.

Some of the pottery at the Eaker Site is adorned with shell and engraved decorations, indicating trade connections and cultural exchange with other regions.

559.

The Eaker Site is known for the discovery of the famous "Nodena style" pottery, characterized by its distinctive red and white slip decoration.

560.

The Nodena people at the Eaker Site were skilled farmers, cultivating crops such as maize, beans, and squash.

561.

They also relied on hunting, fishing, and gathering for sustenance, taking advantage of the rich resources provided by the Mississippi River and surrounding landscape.

562.

The Eaker Site contains evidence of a complex social structure, with structures such as large ceremonial mounds and residential areas.

563.

The ceremonial mounds found at the Eaker Site were likely used for religious and ceremonial purposes, possibly including the burial of important individuals.

564.

The Nodena people at the Eaker Site practiced a form of mound building, constructing earthworks for both practical and symbolic reasons.

565.

The Eaker Site is considered a significant archaeological find due to its well-preserved cultural materials and its contribution to understanding the Mississippian culture.

566.

The site provides insights into the daily life, social organization, and belief systems of the Nodena people.

567.

Excavations at the Eaker Site have uncovered evidence of long-distance trade networks, with artifacts from distant regions indicating the extent of cultural interaction.

568.

The Eaker Site is part of the Nodena Phase, a period of cultural development within the Late Mississippian period.

569.

The site has helped archaeologists understand the Nodena culture's interactions with other Mississippian cultures, such as the Cahokia and Spiro cultures.

570.

The Eaker Site is managed and preserved by the Arkansas Archeological Survey and is open to the public for educational purposes.

571.

The site offers interpretive panels and exhibits that provide information about the archaeology and history of the region.

572.

The artifacts discovered at the Eaker Site are housed in various museums, including the Arkansas State University Museum and the Parkin Archeological State Park.

573.

The Eaker Site has been extensively studied by archaeologists, contributing to scholarly knowledge about the Mississippian culture and its regional variations.

574.

The site has also been used as a training ground for aspiring archaeologists and students, offering hands-on experience in excavation techniques and artifact analysis.

575.

The Nodena people at the Eaker Site were part of a larger cultural complex known as the Southeastern Ceremonial Complex, which encompassed various Native American groups in the southeastern United States.

576.

The Eaker Site provides evidence of the Nodena people's engagement in ceremonial practices and their connection to the larger religious and cosmological beliefs of the Mississippian culture.

577.

The site's location near the Mississippi River would have provided the Nodena people with access to a major transportation route and trade network.

578.

The Nodena people at the Eaker Site were skilled potters, creating vessels of various shapes and sizes for everyday use and ceremonial purposes.

579.

The pottery found at the Eaker Site has been used to date other archaeological sites in the region, providing valuable chronological markers for understanding the Mississippian culture.

580.

The Eaker Site is part of a larger network of archaeological sites in the Mississippi River Valley, which collectively contribute to our understanding of pre-Columbian Native American cultures.

581.

The Nodena people at the Eaker Site were skilled in agriculture and practiced advanced techniques such as raised bed gardening and irrigation.

582.

The Eaker Site offers opportunities for visitors to learn about the history and culture of the Nodena people through guided tours and interpretive programs.

583.

The site's location near the Mississippi River provides a scenic backdrop for visitors, allowing them to appreciate the natural beauty of the region.

584.

The Eaker Site has been featured in archaeological publications and scholarly articles, contributing to the broader field of Mississippian archaeology.

585.

The site's excavation and research have involved collaboration between archaeologists, historians, tribal representatives, and local communities.

586.

The Eaker Site serves as a reminder of the rich cultural heritage and history of the indigenous peoples who inhabited the region long before European settlement.

587.

The Eaker Site represents a tangible connection to the past, allowing visitors to explore and appreciate the achievements and innovations of the Nodena people.

588.

The site offers a glimpse into the complex societal structure and organization of the Mississippian culture, highlighting their achievements in agriculture, architecture, and art.

589.

The Eaker Site has been designated as a National Historic Landmark, recognizing its importance and significance in American history.

590.

The Nodena culture, represented by the artifacts found at the Eaker Site, had a distinct material culture and artistic style that set them apart from other contemporary Native American groups.

591.

The site's preservation and ongoing research contribute to our understanding of cultural change and continuity over time, shedding light on the dynamics of prehistoric societies.

592.

The Eaker Site has sparked interest and curiosity among the local community, fostering a sense of pride and appreciation for the region's archaeological heritage.

593.

The archaeological work conducted at the Eaker Site has involved careful excavation, documentation, and analysis of artifacts and ecofacts to piece together the story of the Nodena people.

594.

The site's location along the Mississippi River would have provided the Nodena people with access to a diverse range of natural resources, supporting their subsistence and cultural practices.

595.

The artifacts found at the Eaker Site are not only valuable for archaeological research but also serve as a tangible link to the cultural traditions and artistic expressions of the Nodena people.

596.

The Eaker Site's archaeological discoveries have challenged previous assumptions and expanded our understanding of the Mississippian culture and its regional variations.

597.

The site's excavation process involves meticulous record-keeping and the use of advanced scientific techniques to extract as much information as possible from the artifacts and features.

598.

The Eaker Site contributes to ongoing discussions and debates within the field of archaeology, providing new insights into the cultural dynamics and interactions of ancient societies.

599.

The Eaker Site showcases the significance of preserving and protecting archaeological sites to ensure future generations can continue to learn from and appreciate our shared heritage.

600.

The Eaker Site stands as a testament to the ingenuity, creativity, and cultural achievements of the Nodena people, leaving a lasting legacy that continues to fascinate and inspire researchers, visitors, and enthusiasts.

601.

Gilbert Stuart was an American portrait painter born on December 3, 1755, in Saunderstown, Rhode Island.

602.

He was recognized as one of America's foremost portrait painters and became renowned for his depictions of prominent figures, including several U.S. presidents.

603.

Stuart's most famous portrait is the unfinished portrait of George Washington known as "The Athenaeum" or "Lansdowne portrait," which is considered an iconic image of the first U.S. president.

604.

Stuart's father, Gilbert Stuart Sr., was a Scottish immigrant who worked as a snuff grinder, and his mother, Elizabeth Anthony, was of Irish descent.

605.

As a child, Stuart displayed artistic talent and received some informal instruction in painting from his Scottish-born father.

606.

At the age of 14, Stuart left Rhode Island and moved to Newport, where he apprenticed with Scottish painter Cosmo Alexander.

607.

Stuart later moved to London in 1775 to study and further his artistic career.

608.

In London, Stuart became a student of Benjamin West, an influential American painter who had established himself in Britain.

609.

Stuart gained recognition for his portraits and became a sought-after portrait painter among the British aristocracy.

610.

Despite his success in London, Stuart returned to the United States in 1793 and settled in Philadelphia.

611.

In Philadelphia, Stuart quickly established himself as a prominent portrait painter and began receiving commissions from notable figures, including members of the political elite.

612.

Stuart's ability to capture a sitter's likeness and convey their personality through his paintings earned him a reputation as a skilled portraitist.

613.

His portraits were characterized by their meticulous attention to detail, refined technique, and a focus on capturing the essence of the subject.

614.

Stuart's portraits often depicted his subjects in a dignified and elegant manner, reflecting the conventions of the time.

615.

He had a talent for capturing the subtleties of facial expressions and was skilled at conveying the sitter's character and emotions through his brushwork.

616.

Stuart's portraits of George Washington are considered some of the most iconic representations of the first U.S. president.

617.

He painted three different portraits of Washington during his lifetime, and many of the subsequent images of Washington were derived from Stuart's original works.

618.

Stuart's portraits of Washington were known for their powerful presence and their ability to convey Washington's stature and leadership.

619.

Despite his success as a portrait painter, Stuart struggled with financial difficulties throughout his career and was often plagued by debt.

620.

He had a reputation for being an eccentric and unpredictable personality, which sometimes affected his professional relationships and ability to secure commissions.

621.

Stuart had a long-standing rivalry with fellow American portrait painter John Trumbull, and the two often engaged in public disputes and criticism of each other's work.

622.

Stuart's personal life was tumultuous, and he had several failed marriages and numerous children.

623.

One of Stuart's daughters, Jane Stuart, also became a successful portrait painter and studied under her father.

624.

Stuart's work was greatly influenced by European art, particularly the work of the Old Masters such as Anthony van Dyck and Peter Paul Rubens.

625.

He admired the loose brushwork and rich color palettes of these artists and incorporated similar techniques into his own style.

626.

Stuart's portraits captured the spirit of the American Revolution era and contributed to the development of a distinct American school of painting.

627.

His portraits often depicted his subjects with symbols and objects that conveyed their social status, accomplishments, or interests.

628.

Stuart painted portraits of several U.S. presidents, including John Adams, Thomas Jefferson, and James Madison.

629.

His portrait of Thomas Jefferson is notable for its sensitivity and the contemplative expression captured on Jefferson's face.

630.

Stuart's portrait of James Madison, known as the "Munificent Congress" portrait, depicts Madison surrounded by the members of the 1st United States Congress.

631.

Stuart's portraits of women were praised for their grace and beauty, and he was particularly skilled at capturing the delicacy of their features.

632.

Stuart's portrait of Dolley Madison, the wife of President James Madison, is regarded as one of his finest female portraits.

633.

In addition to political figures, Stuart also painted portraits of prominent intellectuals, artists, and socialites of his time.

634.

Stuart's work was sought after by many influential individuals, and he had a significant impact on the development of American portraiture.

635.

Despite his artistic success, Stuart often struggled with deadlines and unfinished commissions, leaving many portraits incomplete.

636.

Stuart's style and approach to portraiture influenced future generations of American artists, and his legacy can be seen in the works of subsequent portrait painters.

637.

His ability to capture the character and essence of his subjects through his paintings set a standard for American portraiture.

638.

Stuart's portraits are now housed in major museums and galleries around the world, including the National Gallery of Art in Washington, D.C., and the Metropolitan Museum of Art in New York City.

639.

He continued to paint portraits until his death, leaving behind a substantial body of work that showcases his talent and contributions to American art.

640.

Stuart's influence on American portraiture can still be felt today, as his techniques and approach continue to inspire contemporary portrait painters.

641.

His legacy extends beyond his artistic achievements, as his portraits serve as important historical records of the figures who shaped early American history.

642.

Stuart's works are highly sought after by collectors, and his portraits command significant prices at auctions and in private sales.

643.

Despite his fame as a portrait painter, Stuart's financial struggles persisted throughout his life, and he often had to rely on the support of friends and patrons to sustain himself.

644.

Stuart's dedication to his craft and commitment to capturing the essence of his subjects earned him the respect and admiration of his contemporaries.

645.

He was a founding member of the Pennsylvania Academy of the Fine Arts and played a role in shaping the early American art scene.

646.

Stuart's legacy as a portrait painter is celebrated and revered, and his contributions to American art continue to be studied and appreciated by art historians and enthusiasts.

647.

His impact on the art world was recognized during his lifetime, and he was honored with numerous awards and accolades.

648.

Stuart's work has been featured in major exhibitions, and retrospectives of his art have been organized to commemorate his artistic achievements.

649.

The Gilbert Stuart Birthplace and Museum, located in Saunderstown, Rhode Island, preserves the house where Stuart was born and showcases a collection of his works.

650.

Stuart's artistic talent, perseverance, and dedication to his craft have solidified his place as one of America's most important portrait painters, leaving a lasting legacy in the world of art.

651.

William Strickland was an American architect born on November 1788 in Navesink, New Jersey.

652.

He is known for his contributions to the Greek Revival architectural style in the United States.

653.

Strickland began his career as a carpenter and joiner before transitioning to architecture.

654.

He studied architecture under Benjamin Latrobe, one of the most prominent architects of the time.

655.

Strickland's early works were mainly focused on designing and constructing houses and churches in the Philadelphia area.

656.

He gained recognition for his design of the Second Bank of the United States in Philadelphia, completed in 1824.

657.

The Second Bank of the United States is considered one of Strickland's most significant works and is recognized as a masterpiece of Greek Revival architecture.

658.

Strickland's design for the Second Bank of the United States featured a monumental Greek temple façade with Doric columns and a prominent pediment.

659.

He was also responsible for designing the Merchants' Exchange in Philadelphia, completed in 1834, which became an iconic symbol of the city.

660.

The Merchants' Exchange is known for its impressive Greek Revival portico and grand interior spaces.

661.

Strickland designed numerous churches in Philadelphia, including St. Stephen's Episcopal Church and the First Unitarian Church, which showcased his talent for blending classical architectural elements with religious symbolism.

662.

He also designed the United States Naval Asylum in Philadelphia, now known as the Naval Home, which served as a retirement home for naval veterans.

663.

Strickland's designs were characterized by their symmetry, proportion, and use of classical ornamentation, reflecting the influence of Greek and Roman architecture.

664.

He was one of the first American architects to fully embrace the Greek Revival style, helping to popularize it across the country.

665.

Strickland's architectural designs extended beyond Philadelphia, with notable works in other cities such as Baltimore, New York, and Nashville.

666.

In Baltimore, he designed the St. Paul's Episcopal Church, which featured a distinctive octagonal tower and a classically inspired interior.

667.

Strickland's design for the Tennessee State Capitol in Nashville, completed in 1859, is considered one of his most significant works outside of Philadelphia.

668.

The Tennessee State Capitol showcases Strickland's mastery of the Greek Revival style and remains a prominent landmark in the city.

669.

Strickland was highly sought after as an architect and received commissions from various government, religious, and civic institutions.

670.

He was a founding member of the American Institute of Architects, established in 1857, and played a role in advancing the architectural profession in the United States.

671.

Strickland's architectural designs were influenced by the principles of the Greek classical orders, with an emphasis on harmony, proportion, and simplicity.

672.

He believed that architecture should be based on universal principles and sought to create buildings that would stand the test of time.

673.

Strickland was known for his attention to detail and meticulous craftsmanship, ensuring that his buildings were executed with precision and quality.

674.

He often collaborated with skilled craftsmen and artisans to realize his architectural visions.

675.

Strickland's designs ranged from small-scale residential buildings to large public structures, demonstrating his versatility as an architect.

676.

He was particularly skilled at adapting classical architectural elements to suit the needs and functions of his buildings.

677.

Strickland's designs contributed to the architectural landscape of the United States during a period of rapid urbanization and expansion.

678.

His work helped shape the aesthetic and cultural identity of American cities, especially in the early to mid-19th century.

679.

Strickland's designs were influential and inspired other architects of his time and subsequent generations.

680.

He had a significant impact on the development of Greek Revival architecture in the United States, which became a dominant architectural style during the period.

681.

Strickland's architectural drawings and plans were meticulously detailed and served as valuable records of his designs and construction techniques.

682.

He often incorporated advanced engineering principles into his buildings, ensuring their structural stability and longevity.

683.

Strickland's designs were not limited to public and religious buildings. He also created residential designs, including grand mansions for wealthy clients.

684.

He believed that architecture should be accessible to all and advocated for the use of classical forms in public buildings to inspire civic pride.

685.

Strickland's work was influenced by the architectural styles of ancient Greece and Rome, as well as the Neoclassical movement in Europe.

686.

He made several trips to Europe, where he studied classical architecture firsthand and drew inspiration from notable buildings and monuments.

687.

Strickland's commitment to the Greek Revival style sometimes drew criticism from those who favored other architectural styles or advocated for a more uniquely American approach.

688.

Despite the criticism, Strickland remained dedicated to the Greek Revival style throughout his career and continued to refine and evolve his designs within its framework.

689.

He believed that the Greek Revival style represented the ideals of democracy and civic virtue, making it particularly appropriate for public buildings.

690.

Strickland's architectural designs were praised for their elegance, grace, and timelessness.

691.

He was known for his ability to create buildings that were both aesthetically pleasing and functional, meeting the needs of their occupants and users.

692.

Strickland's influence extended beyond his lifetime, as his designs continued to inspire architects in the generations that followed.

693.

His architectural legacy can be seen in the numerous Greek Revival buildings that still exist across the United States.

694.

Strickland's contributions to American architecture were recognized during his lifetime, and he received accolades and awards for his work.

695.

He was dedicated to promoting architectural education and served as a mentor to aspiring architects, sharing his knowledge and expertise.

696.

Strickland's architectural practice was a family affair, with his son, Walter, joining him in the profession and later taking over the firm.

697.

His son, Walter Strickland, continued the family legacy and contributed to the architectural landscape of Philadelphia and beyond.

698.

Strickland's architectural drawings and sketches are held in various collections and archives, providing valuable insights into his design process and thinking.

699.

His work continues to be studied and appreciated by architectural historians and enthusiasts, who recognize his significant contributions to American architecture.

700.

Strickland's commitment to the Greek Revival style and his dedication to creating buildings of enduring beauty and significance have solidified his place as one of the most influential architects in American history.

701.

The British water vole, also known as the European water vole (Arvicola amphibius), is a semi-aquatic rodent native to the British Isles.

702.

It is the largest vole species found in the UK, with adults typically measuring around 20-25 cm in length, excluding the tail.

703.

Water voles have a stout, rounded body, short legs, and a blunt nose. Their fur is dense and usually brown with a lighter underside.

704.

They are excellent swimmers and spend a significant amount of time in the water, using their webbed feet and strong tails to navigate through streams, rivers, and ponds.

705.

Water voles are herbivores, primarily feeding on a diet of grasses, sedges, and other aquatic vegetation.

706.

They are active during the day and are most commonly seen near the water's edge, where they forage for food and construct burrows.

707.

Water voles are skilled burrowers and create elaborate tunnel systems in the banks of rivers, ditches, and ponds. These burrows provide them with shelter, protection from predators, and nesting sites.

708.

The burrows of water voles can be recognized by their characteristic "lawns" or grazed areas of vegetation around the burrow entrances.

709.

Water voles are social animals and live in small family groups. A typical group consists of a breeding male, one or more breeding females, and their offspring.

710.

Breeding season for water voles typically occurs from March to October, with females producing multiple litters per year.

711.

After a gestation period of around 20 days, the female water vole gives birth to a litter of 3 to 5 young, known as pups.

712.

The pups are born blind and hairless but develop quickly. They start venturing outside the burrow at around two weeks old and become independent at about one month.

713.

Water voles have a lifespan of around one to two years in the wild, although some individuals may live longer.

714.

The British water vole is an excellent swimmer, capable of staying submerged for up to 30 seconds.

715.

Water voles communicate through a range of vocalizations, including high-pitched squeaks, chirps, and growls.

716.

Their natural predators include birds of prey, such as owls and kestrels, as well as carnivorous mammals like stoats, weasels, and mink.

717.

The decline of water voles in the UK has been largely attributed to predation by non-native American mink, which were introduced for fur farming and have become invasive.

718.

Conservation efforts have been made to protect water voles and their habitats. Initiatives include habitat restoration, mink control programs, and captive breeding programs.

719.

Water voles are protected by law in the UK under the Wildlife and Countryside Act 1981, making it illegal to intentionally kill or disturb them or their habitats.

720.

Their decline in numbers led to water voles being listed as a priority species for conservation in the UK Biodiversity Action Plan.

721.

Water voles are excellent climbers and can ascend vertical surfaces, using their sharp claws to grip onto vegetation or tree trunks.

722.

They are known for their impressive swimming speed, reaching up to 5 km/h (3 mph) in the water.

723.

Water voles are primarily active during the warmer months, but they do not hibernate and remain active throughout the winter.

724.

The teeth of water voles continually grow throughout their lives, allowing them to gnaw on vegetation and keep their teeth in good condition.

725.

The fur of water voles is specially adapted to keep them warm in the water. It traps air bubbles, providing insulation and buoyancy.

726.

Water voles are excellent at tunneling and can excavate burrows up to 2 meters long, creating a network of interconnected passages.

727.

They are territorial animals and mark their territories with scent markings to communicate with other water voles and deter intruders.

728.

The British water vole is a distinct sub-species of the European water vole and is endemic to the British Isles.

729.

Water voles have poor eyesight but possess a keen sense of smell and hearing, which helps them detect predators and locate food.

730.

They are generally non-aggressive animals and tend to avoid confrontations with other water voles or animals.

731.

Water voles are excellent swimmers but are not as proficient on land. They have a distinctive loping gait and may appear clumsy when moving on solid ground.

732.

The British water vole is considered an important indicator of the health of freshwater habitats in the UK.

733.

Water voles play a crucial role in shaping the structure and dynamics of wetland ecosystems through their feeding and burrowing activities.

734.

Their burrows provide shelter and nesting sites for other animals, such as amphibians and invertebrates.

735.

Water voles are excellent ecosystem engineers, altering the landscape through their burrowing and grazing activities, which can create diverse habitats and promote biodiversity.

736.

The presence of water voles in an area is often seen as an indicator of good water quality and a healthy ecosystem.

737.

Water voles are known for their ability to reproduce rapidly, with populations capable of recovering quickly if suitable habitat conditions are restored.

738.

They have a high reproductive potential, with females able to produce several litters in a single breeding season.

739.

Water voles are known by various regional names in the UK, including "water rats," "waterdogs," "water toads," and "bankers."

740.

The decline of water voles in the UK has led to increased conservation efforts, including the creation of "vole-friendly" habitats and the reintroduction of captive-bred individuals to suitable sites.

741.

Water voles are excellent foragers and can consume up to 80% of their body weight in vegetation each day.

742.

They play a crucial role in controlling the growth of aquatic vegetation by feeding on grasses and plants that grow near the water's edge.

743.

The British water vole is an important cultural and literary symbol in the UK, often associated with the character "Ratty" from Kenneth Grahame's classic children's book, "The Wind in the Willows."

744.

Water voles are known to exhibit communal latrines near their burrows, which helps minimize the scent markings within their territories.

745.

Their populations can fluctuate significantly in response to changes in habitat conditions, water levels, and food availability.

746.

Water voles have been successfully reintroduced to several sites across the UK, contributing to their conservation and population recovery efforts.

747.

The reintroduction of water voles often involves habitat restoration and the removal of non-native predators, such as mink, to create suitable conditions for their survival.

748.

The conservation status of water voles varies across different regions of the UK, with some populations showing signs of recovery while others remain at risk.

749.

Water voles are adept at camouflage and can blend seamlessly with their surroundings, making them difficult to spot in their natural habitats.

750.

The British water vole remains an iconic and cherished species in the UK, highlighting the importance of conserving our wetland ecosystems and protecting their habitats.

751.

The British wildcat, also known as the Scottish wildcat (Felis silvestris grampia), is a subspecies of the European wildcat and is native to the British Isles.

752.

It is one of the most endangered mammals in the UK and is considered a priority species for conservation.

753.

The British wildcat is a medium-sized felid, similar in size to a domestic cat but with a more robust build. Adult males can weigh between 5-8 kg, while females are slightly smaller.

754.

They have a distinctively thick, bushy tail with a black tip, which helps with balance and communication.

755.

The fur of the British wildcat is dense and usually grayish-brown with dark stripes or spots, providing excellent camouflage in their natural habitat.

756.

They have a rounded head with prominent cheekbones and tufted ears, which serve as a visual signal to communicate with other wildcats.

757.

British wildcats have a solitary nature and are generally territorial, with each individual occupying a specific range.

758.

Their territories can vary in size but typically cover several square kilometers, depending on the availability of prey and suitable habitat.

759.

British wildcats are primarily nocturnal, meaning they are most active during the night, but they may also be active during dawn and dusk.

760.

They are skilled hunters and primarily prey on small mammals such as rabbits, voles, and mice. Occasionally, they may also catch birds and other small prey.

761.

British wildcats are excellent climbers and have the ability to climb trees to hunt or seek refuge.

762.

They are well-adapted to their environment and can endure harsh weather conditions, including cold winters and wet habitats.

763.

The British wildcat was once distributed throughout the British Isles, but its range has significantly diminished over the years due to habitat loss and human activities.

764.

Today, the remaining populations of British wildcats are predominantly found in the Scottish Highlands and some surrounding areas.

765.

They prefer habitats such as woodland, forest edges, and moorland, which provide cover for hunting and suitable denning sites.

766.

British wildcats are known for their elusive nature and are rarely seen in the wild, making them a challenging species to study and conserve.

767.

The British wildcat is a protected species in the UK, and it is illegal to harm, capture, or kill them.

768.

The major threats to British wildcats include habitat fragmentation, road mortality, hybridization with domestic cats, and diseases transmitted by domestic cats.

769.

Due to its endangered status, conservation efforts are underway to protect and preserve the remaining populations of British wildcats.

770.

Conservation organizations and government agencies are working together to implement measures such as habitat restoration, predator control, and captive breeding programs to support the recovery of the species.

771.

British wildcats are genetically distinct from domestic cats, and it is crucial to prevent hybridization between the two species to maintain the genetic integrity of wildcat populations.

772.

They have a complex social structure, with males and females maintaining separate territories and coming together only for mating purposes.

773.

Mating typically occurs during winter, with a gestation period of around 63 days.

774.

The female wildcat gives birth to a litter of usually 2-4 kittens, which are blind and helpless at birth.

775.

The kittens remain in the den for the first few weeks, relying on their mother for milk and protection.

776.

The mother wildcat provides intensive care to her kittens, teaching them essential hunting and survival skills as they grow.

777.

The kittens start exploring their surroundings at around six weeks old and become independent at around six to eight months.

778.

British wildcats have a lifespan of around 10-12 years in the wild.

779.

They communicate using a variety of vocalizations, including growls, hisses, and purrs, to communicate with other wildcats.

780.

Scent marking is an essential behavior for British wildcats. They use scent glands located on their cheeks, paws, and tails to mark their territories and communicate with other individuals.

781.

British wildcats are known for their agility and speed, which allows them to pursue and capture prey efficiently.

782.

They have sharp retractable claws and powerful jaws, which aid in hunting and catching their prey.

783.

British wildcats are excellent swimmers and are known to cross rivers and streams when necessary.

784.

Despite their name, British wildcats are not exclusive to Scotland. Historically, they were distributed throughout England, Wales, and other parts of the British Isles.

785.

British wildcats are an important part of the ecosystem, helping regulate the populations of their prey species.

786.

The decline of the British wildcat is often attributed to human activities, such as habitat destruction, intensive agriculture, and persecution.

787.

There is ongoing debate among experts regarding the taxonomic classification of the British wildcat, with some considering it a distinct species separate from the European wildcat.

788.

Efforts are being made to raise awareness about the conservation needs of British wildcats and involve local communities in their protection.

789.

Remote camera traps and genetic analysis techniques are used to study and monitor wildcat populations without direct human interference.

790.

Wildlife corridors and habitat connectivity projects are being established to create suitable habitats and ensure the genetic exchange between wildcat populations.

791.

The British wildcat is an iconic symbol of British wildlife and is often featured in folklore, literature, and art.

792.

The European Wildcat Conservation Organization (EWCO) is actively involved in the conservation of wildcats, including the British wildcat.

793.

The conservation of British wildcats is a complex task that requires a multidisciplinary approach involving ecologists, geneticists, conservationists, and local communities.

794.

Climate change and its impact on habitats, prey availability, and disease dynamics may pose additional challenges for the long-term survival of the British wildcat.

795.

The British wildcat has a cultural significance in Scotland and is considered a national symbol of wildlife conservation.

796.

Educational programs and initiatives are being implemented to raise awareness about the importance of conserving British wildcats and their habitats.

797.

The British wildcat is known for its strong instincts and resilience in adapting to challenging environments.

798.

Their presence in an ecosystem indicates the health and biodiversity of the area.

799.

Efforts are being made to integrate scientific research, conservation actions, and local knowledge to develop effective strategies for the protection of British wildcats.

800.

The conservation of British wildcats is a shared responsibility, requiring cooperation and support from individuals, communities, organizations, and governments to ensure their survival for future generations.

801.

Fort Smith is a city located in western Arkansas, United States, at the confluence of the Arkansas and Poteau Rivers.

802.

The city was founded in 1817 as a frontier military post and served as a key outpost during the settlement of the American West.

803.

It was named after General Thomas A. Smith, who commanded the military forces in the area during its early years.

804.

Fort Smith played a crucial role in the Indian Territory, serving as a center for military operations, law enforcement, and trade.

805.

The city served as a hub for the Western frontier, providing supplies, protection, and a base for expeditions into the uncharted territories.

806.

Fort Smith was an important stop along the Trail of Tears, the forced relocation of Native American tribes, including the Cherokee, Choctaw, and Chickasaw, to Indian Territory.

807.

The historic Fort Smith National Historic Site preserves the remains of the original fort and showcases the history of the area.

808.

Fort Smith was an essential military post during the American Civil War, changing hands several times between Union and Confederate forces.

809.

The infamous Judge Isaac Parker, known as the "Hanging Judge," presided over the U.S. District Court in Fort Smith from 1875 to 1896. He was responsible for bringing law and order to the region.

810.

The courtroom where Judge Parker held his trials is now part of the Fort Smith National Historic Site and can be visited by the public.

811.

Fort Smith was a rough and lawless town during its early years, with a reputation for violence and gambling.

812.

In 1896, the United States Army decommissioned the fort, and it was subsequently used as a federal prison.

813.

The federal prison in Fort Smith was known for housing some notorious outlaws, including the famous bank robber, George "Baby Face" Nelson.

814.

The federal prison closed in 1896 and was eventually converted into a courthouse and offices for federal agencies.

815.

Today, the Fort Smith National Historic Site encompasses the historic buildings of the original fort, including barracks, officer quarters, and the gallows used during Judge Parker's era.

816.

The Belle Grove Historic District in Fort Smith is known for its beautiful Victorian-era homes and is listed on the National Register of Historic Places.

817.

Fort Smith played a significant role in the development of the cattle industry in the late 19th century. It served as a trading post and shipping point for cattle drives along the Chisholm Trail.

818.

The city experienced a period of economic growth and prosperity during the early 20th century due to its location as a transportation hub.

819.

The Fort Smith Trolley Museum preserves and operates a collection of historic streetcars, showcasing the city's transportation history.

820.

The Fort Smith Regional Airport provides air travel services to the region, connecting the city to major destinations across the United States.

821.

Fort Smith is home to the University of Arkansas - Fort Smith, offering a variety of undergraduate and graduate programs.

822.

The city is known for its vibrant arts scene, with several galleries, theaters, and cultural events held throughout the year.

823.

The Fort Smith Symphony, founded in 1923, is one of the oldest symphony orchestras in the southern United States.

824.

Fort Smith is situated in the scenic Arkansas River Valley, surrounded by picturesque landscapes, including mountains, forests, and rivers.

825.

The Janet Huckabee Arkansas River Valley Nature Center offers visitors the opportunity to explore and learn about the region's diverse wildlife and natural habitats.

826.

Fort Smith is home to a variety of parks and recreational areas, providing opportunities for outdoor activities such as hiking, fishing, and boating.

827.

The Parrot Island Waterpark is a popular attraction in Fort Smith, offering water slides, lazy rivers, and other fun activities for all ages.

828.

The Fort Smith Convention Center hosts a range of events, including conferences, conventions, concerts, and trade shows.

829.

The city has a rich musical heritage, with notable musicians and bands originating from Fort Smith, including the famous country singer, Johnny Cash.

830.

The Clayton House, a beautiful Victorian mansion, is open to the public and showcases the lifestyle of one of Fort Smith's prominent families in the 19th century.

831.

The Fort Smith Museum of History features exhibits and artifacts that highlight the city's history, culture, and diverse communities.

832.

The annual Old Fort Days Rodeo is a popular event in Fort Smith, attracting participants and spectators from across the country.

833.

The Fort Smith Little Theatre has been entertaining audiences since 1947, presenting a variety of theatrical performances throughout the year.

834.

Fort Smith is known for its friendly and welcoming community, often referred to as "The City of Gracious Living."

835.

The Riverfront Blues Festival, held annually in Fort Smith, showcases local and regional blues musicians and attracts music enthusiasts from all over.

836.

Fort Smith is home to several golf courses, offering challenging fairways and scenic views for golf enthusiasts.

837.

The Fort Smith Farmers Market provides a venue for local farmers and artisans to sell their fresh produce, crafts, and homemade goods.

838.

The Fort Smith Regional Art Museum exhibits a diverse collection of artworks from local, regional, and national artists.

839.

The city has a thriving culinary scene, with a wide range of restaurants offering diverse cuisines, from Southern comfort food to international flavors.

840.

Fort Smith is known for its strong sense of community and volunteerism, with many residents actively involved in charitable organizations and community projects.

841.

The Fort Smith Airshow, held periodically, showcases impressive aerial displays by military and civilian aircraft, attracting aviation enthusiasts from around the region.

842.

The Fort Smith National Cemetery is the final resting place for many veterans, including those who served in the Civil War, World War I, World War II, and subsequent conflicts.

843.

Fort Smith is home to the U.S. Marshals Museum, which honors the legacy and history of the United States Marshals Service.

844.

The city hosts various festivals and events throughout the year, including the Fort Smith Riverfront Blues Fest, the Peacemaker Music and Arts Festival, and the Fort Smith Marathon.

845.

Fort Smith's location on the Arkansas River offers opportunities for recreational boating, including fishing, kayaking, and paddleboarding.

846.

The Fort Smith Public Library system provides a wide range of resources, programs, and services to the community.

847.

The city has a strong sports culture, with local teams and organizations offering opportunities for participation and competition in various sports.

848.

Fort Smith is home to a vibrant downtown area, featuring historic buildings, shopping districts, restaurants, and entertainment venues.

849.

The Fort Smith Regional Art Center offers art classes, workshops, and exhibitions, promoting artistic expression and creativity in the community.

850.

Fort Smith continues to evolve and grow while preserving its rich history and cultural heritage, making it a unique and dynamic city in the heart of Arkansas.

851.

The Menard-Hodges site is an archaeological site located in Monroe County, Arkansas, United States.

852.

It is situated along the White River and covers an area of approximately 24 acres.

853.

The site was first occupied by Native American cultures around 1000-1300 AD during the Late Mississippian period.

854.

Excavations at the Menard-Hodges site have revealed a wealth of artifacts and structures, providing valuable insights into the lives of the people who lived there.

855.

The site features several earthen mounds, including a central platform mound and smaller residential mounds.

856.

The central platform mound at the Menard-Hodges site is one of the largest in the region, standing approximately 30 feet high.

857.

The purpose of the platform mound was likely ceremonial, serving as a focal point for religious and social activities.

858.

The mounds at the Menard-Hodges site were constructed using a combination of earth and clay, shaped into distinct layers to create a stable structure.

859.

The site also includes evidence of a palisade wall, a defensive structure made of wooden posts, which surrounded the settlement.

860.

The palisade wall provided protection to the inhabitants and helped define the boundaries of the community.

861.

Archaeologists have uncovered evidence of houses and other structures within the site, indicating a complex and organized settlement.

862.

The houses at the Menard-Hodges site were typically made of wattle and daub, with wooden frames and walls constructed from woven branches and covered in a mixture of clay and mud.

863.

The site has yielded a wide range of artifacts, including pottery, stone tools, bone tools, shell ornaments, and pottery.

864.

The pottery found at the Menard-Hodges site exhibits intricate designs and decorations, reflecting the artistic and cultural skills of the inhabitants.

865.

The artifacts suggest a reliance on agriculture, with evidence of corn cultivation and the use of farming tools such as hoes.

866.

The people of the Menard-Hodges site engaged in trade and exchange networks, as indicated by the presence of exotic artifacts, such as marine shells and copper objects, which were not locally available.

867.

The site's location along the White River provided easy access to water resources, including fish, shellfish, and waterfowl, contributing to the subsistence strategies of the inhabitants.

868.

The Menard-Hodges site is part of a larger complex of Mississippian settlements in the area, suggesting interconnected social and economic relationships.

869.

The site was inhabited for several centuries before being abandoned, likely due to changes in social, economic, or environmental factors.

870.

The Menard-Hodges site was rediscovered and investigated by archaeologists in the 1970s, leading to significant findings and a better understanding of the Mississippian culture in the region.

871.

The site is listed on the National Register of Historic Places, recognizing its historical and archaeological significance.

872.

The Menard-Hodges site is considered an important archaeological site for studying the development and organization of Mississippian societies in the southeastern United States.

873.

Excavations and research conducted at the site have contributed to our understanding of prehistoric Native American cultures and their interactions in the region.

874.

The Menard-Hodges site provides valuable data for studying settlement patterns, architecture, subsistence strategies, and social organization during the Late Mississippian period.

875.

The archaeological work at the Menard-Hodges site has involved the collaboration of researchers, archaeologists, and local communities to preserve and interpret the site's cultural heritage.

876.

The artifacts recovered from the site are curated and displayed in museums, contributing to public education and awareness of the region's rich archaeological heritage.

877.

The Menard-Hodges site serves as a reminder of the diverse and complex societies that existed in prehistoric Arkansas and their enduring influence on the region's history.

878.

The site's preservation and ongoing research provide opportunities for future generations to learn about and appreciate the cultural legacy of the people who once inhabited the area.

879.

The Menard-Hodges site offers a glimpse into the daily lives, traditions, and beliefs of the Native American communities that thrived in the region centuries ago.

880.

The excavation and interpretation of the Menard-Hodges site continue to contribute to the broader field of archaeology and the understanding of indigenous cultures in North America.

881.

The study of the Menard-Hodges site sheds light on the Mississippian religious practices, social hierarchies, and community interactions.

882.

The preservation and protection of the Menard-Hodges site contribute to the conservation of Arkansas's cultural heritage and the recognition of its archaeological importance.

883.

The Menard-Hodges site offers opportunities for archaeological field schools, where students and researchers can gain hands-on experience in excavation techniques and data analysis.

884.

The Menard-Hodges site is part of a larger effort to document and preserve the archaeological sites of the White River Valley, fostering a greater understanding of the region's past.

885.

The Menard-Hodges site serves as a reminder of the resilience and adaptability of indigenous peoples in the face of environmental and social changes.

886.

The archaeological investigations at the Menard-Hodges site have helped debunk misconceptions and stereotypes about prehistoric Native American cultures, emphasizing their complexity and sophistication.

887.

The Menard-Hodges site provides opportunities for public engagement through guided tours, educational programs, and outreach initiatives that promote the appreciation and stewardship of cultural heritage.

888.

The Menard-Hodges site contributes to the broader narrative of Native American history in Arkansas, connecting past and present communities.

889.

The study of the Menard-Hodges site continues to generate new research questions and avenues of inquiry, stimulating further archaeological investigations in the region.

890.

The Menard-Hodges site showcases the expertise and interdisciplinary collaboration among archaeologists, anthropologists, historians, and tribal communities in unraveling the mysteries of the past.

891.

The Menard-Hodges site has been a source of inspiration for artists, writers, and filmmakers, who draw upon its historical and cultural significance in their creative works.

892.

The Menard-Hodges site serves as a valuable resource for comparative studies, enabling researchers to draw connections and make broader interpretations about Mississippian societies across the southeastern United States.

893.

The preservation of the Menard-Hodges site contributes to the economic vitality of the region by attracting tourists, researchers, and scholars interested in exploring its rich cultural heritage.

894.

The Menard-Hodges site showcases the importance of archaeological conservation and the need for responsible stewardship of our shared cultural resources.

895.

The Menard-Hodges site provides opportunities for collaborative research projects between academic institutions, Native American tribes, and local communities, fostering a deeper understanding of the region's history.

896.

The excavation techniques used at the Menard-Hodges site have evolved over time, incorporating advanced technologies and methodologies to extract and analyze archaeological data with precision.

897.

The Menard-Hodges site has been used as a case study for understanding long-term cultural changes, such as population movements, trade networks, and sociopolitical shifts.

898.

The Menard-Hodges site represents a testament to the resilience and adaptability of the Native American cultures that once flourished in the area.

899.

The Menard-Hodges site provides a platform for cultural exchange and collaboration between archaeologists and descendant communities, fostering mutual understanding and respect.

900.

The Menard-Hodges site stands as a reminder of the diverse and complex tapestry of human history, encouraging us to reflect on our shared past and the significance of preserving our archaeological heritage for future generations.

901.

The Nodena site is an archaeological site located in northeastern Arkansas, United States.

902.

It was occupied by Native American cultures from approximately 1400 to 1650 AD during the Late Mississippian period.

903.

The site covers an area of approximately 32 acres and is situated along the Mississippi River.

904.

The Nodena site is known for its unique artifacts, including the famous Nodena-style pottery, which is characterized by intricate shell-tempered designs.

905.

Excavations at the Nodena site have revealed a complex of earthen mounds and residential areas, indicating a well-organized and thriving settlement.

906.

The largest mound at the Nodena site, known as Mound C, is approximately 25 feet high and served as a platform for ceremonial and religious activities.

907.

The Nodena site was a significant trade and cultural center, with evidence of trade connections reaching as far as the Gulf Coast and the Great Lakes region.

908.

The site's strategic location along the Mississippi River allowed for easy transportation and facilitated extensive trade networks.

909.

The Nodena site features evidence of a palisade wall surrounding the settlement, providing protection and delineating the boundaries of the community.

910.

The inhabitants of the Nodena site relied on agriculture, cultivating crops such as corn, beans, and squash.

911.

The site has yielded a wide range of artifacts, including stone tools, bone tools, copper ornaments, shell beads, and clay figurines.

912.

The clay figurines found at the Nodena site depict various human and animal forms, showcasing the artistic skills and cultural expressions of the inhabitants.

913.

Excavations at the Nodena site have uncovered evidence of a highly stratified society, with indications of social hierarchies and ceremonial activities associated with the ruling elite.

914.

The Nodena site is famous for the discovery of a mass burial mound containing the remains of individuals who may have been sacrificial victims or members of the ruling class.

915.

The burial mound at the Nodena site provides valuable insights into the religious and ritual practices of the Mississippian people.

916.

The site also includes evidence of a large ceremonial plaza, which served as a gathering place for communal activities and public events.

917.

The Nodena site is believed to have been abandoned around 1650 AD, possibly due to environmental changes, social upheaval, or conflict.

918.

The archaeological work at the Nodena site began in the 1930s and continues to the present day, contributing to our understanding of Mississippian culture in the region.

919.

The artifacts recovered from the Nodena site are curated and displayed in museums, providing opportunities for public education and appreciation of the site's cultural heritage.

920.

The Nodena site is listed on the National Register of Historic Places, recognizing its historical and archaeological significance.

921.

The study of the Nodena site has shed light on the interactions between Mississippian societies across the southeastern United States.

922.

The Nodena site has been a subject of research and collaboration between archaeologists, anthropologists, historians, and tribal communities, fostering a greater understanding of the region's past.

923.

The pottery from the Nodena site has become an iconic representation of Mississippian culture and is highly sought after by collectors and enthusiasts.

924.

The Nodena site is considered a key archaeological site for understanding the development and organization of Mississippian societies in the Mississippi River Valley.

925.

The site's preservation and ongoing research contribute to the conservation of Arkansas's cultural heritage and the recognition of its archaeological importance.

926.

The Nodena site provides opportunities for field schools and archaeological training programs, where students and researchers can gain hands-on experience in excavation techniques and data analysis.

927.

The Nodena site has been instrumental in shaping our understanding of the prehistoric Native American cultures in the region, challenging assumptions and stereotypes about their complexity and sophistication.

928.

The artifacts from the Nodena site have been studied using various scientific techniques, including radiocarbon dating and residue analysis, to gain insights into the site's chronology and the activities of its inhabitants.

929.

The Nodena site serves as a case study for examining long-term cultural changes, social interactions, and the impact of environmental factors on ancient societies.

930.

The Nodena site is part of a broader cultural landscape that includes other Mississippian sites, showcasing the interconnectedness and cultural diversity of the region.

931.

The preservation of the Nodena site involves collaboration between archaeologists, government agencies, and local communities to ensure its protection and interpretation for future generations.

932.

The study of the Nodena site has contributed to the development of regional archaeological theories and interpretations, enriching our understanding of the Mississippian period.

933.

The Nodena site has been depicted in art, literature, and popular culture, inspiring creative works that bring attention to its historical and cultural significance.

934.

The Nodena site offers opportunities for public engagement through guided tours, interpretive exhibits, and educational programs that promote awareness and appreciation of the site's archaeological heritage.

935.

The excavation techniques used at the Nodena site have evolved over time, incorporating advanced technologies and methodologies to extract and analyze archaeological data with precision.

936.

The Nodena site represents an important chapter in the history of Native American cultures in Arkansas and serves as a testament to their resilience and adaptability.

937.

The ongoing research at the Nodena site continues to generate new discoveries and knowledge about the people who once inhabited the area, contributing to the broader field of archaeology.

938.

The Nodena site showcases the significance of interdisciplinary collaboration, with researchers from various disciplines working together to unravel the mysteries of the past.

939.

The Nodena site provides a window into the daily lives, belief systems, and cultural practices of the Mississippian people, offering valuable insights into their worldview.

940.

The artifacts and features discovered at the Nodena site are carefully documented and analyzed, contributing to a comprehensive understanding of the site's history and significance.

941.

The Nodena site has been a site of pilgrimage and reverence for Native American communities and serves as a connection to their ancestral heritage.

942.

The Nodena site's location near the Mississippi River emphasizes the importance of rivers as transportation routes and cultural corridors in ancient societies.

943.

The Nodena site provides opportunities for comparative studies, allowing researchers to explore similarities and differences with other Mississippian sites in the southeastern United States.

944.

The Nodena site's artifacts and data contribute to ongoing discussions and debates in archaeology, helping to refine our understanding of past societies and their interactions.

945.

The study of the Nodena site fosters a deeper appreciation for the diversity of Native American cultures and their contributions to the development of the Americas.

946.

The Nodena site serves as a reminder of the continuous occupation of the region by indigenous peoples for thousands of years, challenging narratives that focus solely on European colonial history.

947.

The archaeological investigations at the Nodena site have highlighted the importance of collaboration and consultation with Native American tribes, ensuring their perspectives are incorporated into the research and interpretation process.

948.

The Nodena site stands as a testament to the value of archaeological research in uncovering the hidden stories and experiences of ancient civilizations.

949.

The Nodena site's legacy extends beyond its boundaries, influencing archaeological methodologies and interpretations in the study of Mississippian cultures.

950.

The Nodena site serves as a source of inspiration and curiosity, fueling ongoing research and exploration into the history and heritage of the indigenous peoples who once called the area home.

951.

Matthew Thornton was born on March 17, 1714, in Ireland, and later emigrated to the American colonies.

952.

Thornton was a physician by profession and practiced medicine in New Hampshire.

953.

He graduated from the College of New Jersey (now Princeton University) in 1740 and then studied medicine in Edinburgh, Scotland.

954.

Thornton returned to New Hampshire in 1747 and established a successful medical practice.

955.

In addition to his medical career, Thornton also became involved in politics and public service.

956.

He served as a member of the New Hampshire Provincial Congress and as a justice of the peace.

957.

Thornton was an active participant in the movement for American independence and supported the revolutionary cause.

958.

He was elected as a delegate to the Continental Congress in 1776 and signed the Declaration of Independence on November 4, 1776.

959.

Thornton's signature on the Declaration of Independence is notable for its large size and distinctive handwriting.

960.

He was one of the four delegates from New Hampshire to sign the Declaration.

961.

Thornton was the last signer of the Declaration of Independence to die, passing away on June 24, 1803, at the age of 89.

962.

He served in the Continental Congress for only a brief period and did not play a prominent role in its proceedings.

963.

After signing the Declaration, Thornton returned to his medical practice in New Hampshire.

964.

Thornton was known for his intelligence, wit, and strong principles, which earned him respect among his peers.

965.

He was an advocate for public education and served as a trustee of Dartmouth College.

966.

Thornton was a devout Christian and held strong religious beliefs throughout his life.

967.

He was a supporter of the Federalist Party and was elected as an associate justice of the New Hampshire Superior Court in 1780.

968.

Thornton played a role in shaping the early legal system of New Hampshire through his judicial service.

969.

He was a vocal critic of the Articles of Confederation and supported the adoption of the United States Constitution.

970.

Thornton was elected as a state senator in New Hampshire in 1784 and served in that position for several years.

971.

Despite his political and professional commitments, Thornton remained dedicated to his medical practice and continued to see patients throughout his life.

972.

He was known for his compassion and dedication to providing healthcare to those in need.

973.

Thornton was married to Hannah Jack, and the couple had five children together.

974.

He was a strong advocate for women's rights and believed in the importance of educating girls.

975.

Thornton had a keen interest in astronomy and made astronomical calculations during his spare time.

976.

He was a member of the American Philosophical Society and corresponded with renowned scientists of his time.

977.

Thornton was a vocal opponent of slavery and actively supported the abolitionist movement.

978.

He believed that all individuals should be treated with equality and dignity.

979.

Thornton's contributions to the American Revolution and his role as a signer of the Declaration of Independence have been commemorated in various ways.

980.

There are several schools, parks, and streets named after Matthew Thornton in different parts of the United States.

981.

Thornton's birthplace in Ireland has been marked with a plaque to honor his legacy.

982.

His life and accomplishments have been studied by historians and scholars interested in the American Revolution and the founding of the nation.

983.

Thornton's signature on the Declaration of Independence is considered an important historical artifact and is on display at the National Archives in Washington, D.C.

984.

His commitment to public service and dedication to the well-being of his community serve as an inspiration to future generations.

985.

Thornton's contributions to the field of medicine and his advocacy for public health have had a lasting impact on healthcare in the United States.

986.

His legacy as a physician and statesman continues to be celebrated in New Hampshire, where he is remembered as one of the state's founding fathers.

987.

Thornton's commitment to the principles of liberty, justice, and equality resonate with the values that define the United States.

988.

He believed in the importance of civic engagement and encouraged active participation in the democratic process.

989.

Thornton's support for education and his belief in the power of knowledge reflect his forward-thinking and progressive mindset.

990.

Throughout his life, Thornton remained committed to the cause of American independence and worked towards securing the freedoms and rights of the American people.

991.

He played a role in drafting New Hampshire's state constitution and was involved in shaping the state's governance.

992.

Thornton's contributions to the medical field extended beyond his practice, as he promoted advancements in medical knowledge and techniques.

993.

He was an early advocate for preventive medicine and emphasized the importance of maintaining a healthy lifestyle.

994.

Thornton's dedication to public service and his unwavering commitment to his principles made him a respected figure among his peers.

995.

His experiences as an immigrant to the American colonies influenced his views on religious freedom and the pursuit of opportunity.

996.

Thornton's belief in the power of unity and collaboration was reflected in his support for a strong central government.

997.

He recognized the importance of forging strong alliances among the states to ensure the success and stability of the new nation.

998.

Thornton's contributions to the field of law and his understanding of the principles of justice and fairness helped shape the legal system of New Hampshire.

999.

His commitment to the well-being of his fellow citizens extended beyond his medical practice, as he actively participated in community-building initiatives.

1000.

Thornton's life and legacy serve as a reminder of the bravery, dedication, and sacrifices of the individuals who laid the foundation for the United States of America.